THE PUSH

120 DEVOTIONS
To Push You Into Purpose

Pastor Margo M. Gross

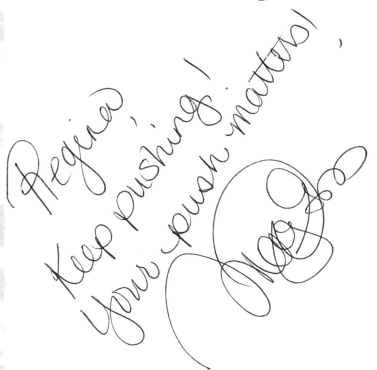

Regina,
Keep pushing !
Your push matters!

ISBN 978-0-692-10748-5
LCCN #: 2018904593

Printed in USA by (Margo M. Gross)

Dedication

With a heart of joy, love, and gratitude, I give all honor to God and dedicate this devotional to my two daughters, Ariyanna and Samiah. May the word of God be forever planted in your hearts. Let His truth light your path. I pray that your faith pushes you beyond all your fears and doubts. Keep pushing. Mommy loves you.

With all my love!
-Mommy

INTRODUCTION

LET THE JOURNEY BEGIN

As we seek to fulfill our purpose in life, it is easy to become distracted, overwhelmed by the obstacles, and discouraged by our mistakes. Maybe you have no idea of your purpose or perhaps you are sure of your purpose. This devotional provides encouragement and discipline, that will push you out of your current comfort zone. In its pages, you will find methods for overcoming some of the most common obstacles to mediocrity; fear, disobedience, and unforgiveness. Themes also include the development of vision, goals, and the importance and posture of transitioning as it relates to your personal journey.

The Push is designed to be read day by day. Reading the devotional page by page, provides an assortment of themes and topics and allows you to navigate through the book one day at a time in order or topically. Reading the entire devotional along with the featured passages of scripture will inspire, encourage, and kick-start you into a productive and purposeful day.

As you work through this devotional, resist the urge to read multiple days or skip the scripture reading. Taking the time to think on each day's message and letting the word of God feed your spirit is essential to attaining the results you seek. All scriptures noted are from the Holy Bible, King James Version (KJV). You should have your bible handy as you embark on your journey.

Finally, The Push has some special features designed to help you have an interactive experience. Each day features a hashtag. The hashtag is designed to help you share your daily experiences with friends and family through social media. In addition, you can connect with others who are also pushing and pursuing. Each day also features a Reflect, Pray, and Plan space. This space is designed to help you reflect and think of personal applications, write specific prayer request(s), and make plans for your next steps. Don't skip this process! By reflecting, praying, and planning, you can apply the word of God and its' message to your life and witness change through the process. There is a decree at the end of each daily devotional. A decree is an official order issued by a legal authority. Every day you must make your decree aloud (in the mirror if possible) with the authority Christ has given you. By making this decree over your day, you begin your day with a positive statement and use the power of your tongue to speak life into your day (Proverbs 18:21 KJV).

At the end of the next four months, you will be pushed into each day with a new sense of purpose as God's word propels you into action and transforms your life. I decree, this devotional and the word of God will aim you as an arrow, shooting you through obstacles, and placing you at your intended target. Be pushed out of your comfort zone and into your purpose!

Margo M. Gross

THE **PUSH**

Day 1 Real Ministry & Purpose
Matthew 6:3-5, 7:17 & 20: 27

Ministry and fulfilling your purpose is not about receiving, taking, and what you can get out of the deal. Ministry is selfless, giving, humbling, and often without reward or fame. Expecting to receive from those we are called to invest in, deposit into, feed, clothe, and protect, can lead to resentment and make you feel unappreciated. While your labor will produce fruit, don't get so caught up in the fruit that you forget to tend to the root! You may find yourself with a dying tree. Be sure to consider what is at the heart of what you do. Motives matter!

#RootDeterminesFruit

Decree: I will use my purpose to give not to take, to heal not to wound, and to help not to hinder.

THE **PUSH**

Pray   **Plan**   **Reflect**

_____
_____
_____
_____
_____
_____
_____
_____
_____
_____
_____
_____
_____
_____
_____
_____
_____
_____
_____
_____
_____
_____
_____
_____
_____
_____
_____
_____
_____
_____
_____

THE **PUSH**

Day 2 Heal So You Can Bear the Weight
First Corinthians 12:12 & Romans 12:4-8

When one part of the body is broken and/or not healed, the rest of the body is affected by the broken and/or not healed parts' inability to perform. The body must bear the weight, shift alignment, and become more productive to compensate. This applies to both the physical body and the church body. We must allow people and things time to heal if we want them to function properly, work effectively, and work in conjunction with the rest of the body. This is especially essential for the load bearing parts of the body. These are our church leaders. Our leaders must walk in healing to bear the weight of those among us who are still in need of healing. The organization would be crippled or hindered from moving forward if the load bearing parts lack the capacity or fortitude to withstand. Healing often requires that you rest and evaluate the body. Sometimes it takes professional therapy. Healing is a process that leads to wholeness. We must rest in God's healing and learn to take the time to rest physically, so we can be a key contributor to the body of Christ.

#HealedNotToHinder

Decree: I have not been broken in any way that God cannot repair. The weight and pressure of my purpose is not too much. With Christ I can bear the weight of my assignment.

THE **PUSH**

Pray   **Plan**   **Reflect**

_____
_____
_____
_____
_____
_____
_____
_____
_____
_____
_____
_____
_____
_____
_____
_____
_____
_____
_____
_____
_____
_____
_____
_____
_____
_____
_____
_____

THE **PUSH**

Day 3 Moving From Like to Love
Mark 12:31 & First Peter 4:8

Moving from like to love! God doesn't ask us to like our neighbors, he says we should love our neighbors as ourselves. Time out for grudges, schisms, making YOUR point, and twisting the word to make our flesh comfortable. Let's love and forgive that we might be forgiven and loved into everlasting life. His promises are not just for you. He is their God too. He came to set the captives free. How dare we pick up the keys and lock others into the same cell of bondage that was opened for us. The key you hold fits your lock too. When you close the gate and turn that lock, it's your prison you have created. If we are trying to fulfill our purpose, we must release others. In releasing them we liberate ourselves.

#Unlocked&Free

Decree: I forgive myself. I forgive others, even if they haven't asked you to forgive them. I let go of everything that holds me back from loving and forgiving. I release everyone from every wrong doing. I walk in freedom that I might free others! I will love as Christ has loved!

6

THE **PUSH**

Pray   **Plan**   **Reflect**

_____

_____

_____

_____

_____

_____

_____

_____

_____

_____

_____

_____

_____

_____

_____

_____

_____

_____

_____

_____

_____

_____

_____

_____

_____

_____

_____

_____

_____

Day 4 Is It Dead or Alive?
Luke 9:60 & Joshua 1:2

Many of us have become pathologists who conduct post-mortem examinations (autopsies) of dead things. We sit wondering why it's dead, investigating what could have gone wrong, and kicking ourselves for not doing enough. Holding on to dead things is not productive. At some point we must shift to become surgeons, skillfully removing things that do not belong, repairing brokenness, and healing scares. We may experience pain and the stress of working on a living body, but at least what we pursue is still alive and has a chance at a better life once it's cut and stitched back together. What is done is done! If you can't change it, let it change you. Learn from it. Put on your scrubs and try fixing the things you can. Let what is dead be buried and leave it there. It won't be a comfortable process, but it will be worth it. Take a few moments to mourn the loss and then move on. In both texts above, the bible tells us that something is dead followed by go and/or get ready. Let the dead bury the dead, while you live.

#FixingWhatICanFix

Decree: Lord, help me to repair what I can and release what I can't change. Today, I bury every dead thing, situation, and circumstance. I eulogize my past, read the obituary of "I can't", and put flowers on the grave of could've and should've. I refuse to be stuck. I bury all dead things and will not dig them up again.

THE **PUSH**

Pray　　　　　　　　　　　**Plan**　　　　　　　　　　　**Reflect**

_____

_____

_____

_____

_____

_____

_____

_____

_____

_____

_____

_____

_____

_____

_____

_____

_____

_____

_____

_____

_____

_____

_____

_____

_____

_____

_____

_____

Day 5 Dangerous Ingredients
First John 2:16 & James 1:14

WARNING! I have observed that lack, opportunity, and vulnerability, operating simultaneously have led many astray. Each of these things operating alone is easier to resist. You may be vulnerable and not given an opportunity. An opportunity may present itself, but during a time when you are not strong. Be careful! Let's not make bad decisions that can have huge impacts on our future to solve temporary dilemma or a desire of the flesh. Don't let loneliness and your desire for attention leave you loveless. What may be lacking is your own security and faith in God. Allow God to conduct a thorough evaluation. You may find that what you thought you needed was always there and avoid chasing what your flesh desires but was never The Lord's will. The choices you make and your ability to make them with a pure heart and clean hands is critical in the pursuit of your purpose.

#DecisionsThatSupportDestiny

Decree: I will not allow lack, vulnerability, and the availability of a counterfeit opportunity, lead me outside of God's will. Lord, protect me from what's not mine.

THE **PUSH**

Pray	Plan	Reflect

Day 6 Baby Steps
James 1:4 & Ecclesiastes 9:11

Sometimes considering the entire project, mission, and assignment can be overwhelming. Consider the process a baby must take to eventually run, jump hurdles, and skip. This all starts with rolling over, crawling, pulling up on furniture, walking, falling, and later running. The baby didn't know it, but its' muscles were being prepared for the run months earlier. The baby receives cheers and claps even when attempts fail! Any journey to a destination is a process. The same way the end goal is broken into smaller steps for the baby, is the same way you can prep for the trip to your promise. Try breaking it down into daily pieces. Celebrate each day's accomplishments and watch it get done slowly, but surely. No city with a firm foundation is built overnight. Every little bit counts. What steps do you need to take to meet your goals and make your dreams come true? Start NOW! Do one thing today.

#BabySteps

Decree: I can accomplish anything through Christ. One day at a time I will meet my goals. Procrastination no longer lives here! I am disciplined, determined, and diligent.

THE **PUSH**

Pray   **Plan**   **Reflect**

Day 7 Wisdom
Proverbs 4:7 & 15:22

When you don't value and solicit constructive feedback, you rob yourself of progression and improvement. Wisdom is the principal thing. Wise counsel is helpful in your journey towards your purpose and destiny. Do you have a mentor who can assist you on this journey? Choose wisely and be in prayer about who and when. Be sure to care more about God's desire for your life than the networking, potential benefits, platforms, or popularity the individual may have. Many have walked the path you're attempting to walk or a similar path. Some have made mistakes and learned valuable lessons that can save you time and effort. Pray for Godly connections and possess wisdom.

#WisdomSeeker

Decree: I will not be intimidated by those who possess what I desire, have developed the skill I need, or have become successful in their fields. I know who I am! Lord, connect me with someone who will know your heart for me without envy or selfish ambition.

THE **PUSH**

Pray   **Plan**   **Reflect**

Day 8 Appreciation
Luke 6:31

With all the things we need to do, have planned, and are busy organizing, it's easy to forget your manners. While you may be hyper focused on your purpose, don't forget to be grateful for those who have helped you. It does not diminish your hard work, or God's hand to acknowledge instrumental people in your purpose process. People do not owe you anything. No one is obligated to be nice. When people consider you, through a kind word, thoughtful gesture or deed, that's a blessing. A little appreciation goes a long way. It is difficult to make it to the next level without some level of assistance. So, say thank you to those who help you because they don't have to consider you. Appreciate those who are hospitable, supportive, and eager to help. Treat people with the same gratitude you wish to receive. Your gifts and talents may take you many places, sit you among many people, but how you treat them will determine how long you stay. The people who work for you are not beneath you in value, they are the foundation of support necessary to hold you up. Remember you were not always who you are now. Remain humble!

Say thank you to someone today! Be grateful!

#MannersOnMyMission

Decree: I will walk in gratitude and thanksgiving daily. I will remain aware that I have been blessed to be a blessing. I will remain humble even when God elevates me. My character will not waiver as I possess my promise.

THE **PUSH**

Pray   **Plan**   **Reflect**

_____

_____

_____

_____

_____

_____

_____

_____

_____

_____

_____

_____

_____

_____

_____

_____

_____

_____

_____

_____

_____

_____

_____

_____

_____

_____

_____

THE **PUSH**

Day 9 Don't Quit
Hebrews 12:1 & Galatians 6:9

The enemy wants you to quit! The battle starts in your mind as the enemy begins to plant seeds of how easy and stress-free life would be if you give up on your dreams and throw in the towel. It then shifts to the physical. You began to become weary and tired in your well doing. Followed by a move to your children, family, spouse, and finances. Ask yourself this question; why is the enemy so focused on his attack towards you? It is because He knows your victory is so close. If you reach out, you can touch it. Take a moment to rest, pray, and maybe even retreat, but don't quit! Muster up that last little bit of "I can make it" and meet me at victory. It's right...... there!

#VictoryIsAfterThis

Decree: I can do all things through Christ Jesus. The finish line is near. I will not give up. The race is given to those who endure. I can make it. I will make it! I was built for this. I am victorious!

THE **PUSH**

Day 10 It's Not Over
Genesis 21: 14-19

What you think is over is just getting started. What you thought was dead is just sleep, and what appears to be an obstacle is merely a stepping stone to strengthen you for the journey to your destiny. Each step making your legs stronger and stronger. Change your perception and see things as they shall be! You are on your way. Consider Hagar. Tossed away after being used, she finds herself without provision for her and her child. It looks like it's over, but in the middle of her wilderness God places a well. A well represents endless provision. Right when you think there is no way, God will make a way in your wilderness.

#InTheWildernessIsAWay

Decree: I'm expecting God to make a way. My faith sees provision, possibility, and the promise! New beginnings and new possibilities belong to me.

THE **PUSH**

Pray   **Plan**   **Reflect**

Day 11 Forward
Philippians 3:13-14

We can become so in love with where we were and where we are that we never get to where we are going. Moving from good to great, requires us to divorce the comforts of predictability. It often means leaving what we know to embark on an unfamiliar journey to where God is calling us. Expect discomfort! Expect your flesh to become intimidated by the vast possibilities, the unknowns, and the unrecognizable scenery along the way. You are traveling on a road many don't travel, going somewhere you've never been. Resist the instinct to get back to the "no faith required zone". In this zone, we operate easily with little resistance from us or others. Push past the resistance to change. Push past the discomfort. PUSH into your purpose!

#PushingIntoPurpose

Decree: I'll do it uncomfortable! I'll conquer new territory! I'll find pleasure in the unfamiliar! I will push!

THE **PUSH**

Pray   **Plan**   **Reflect**

Day 12 Keep, Start, & Stop
Psalms 90:12

Get a piece of paper and a pencil (or write in this devotional). Make three columns; keep, start, and stop. As you pursue your purpose it is essential to take part in self-reflection. This reflection will assist you in managing your time. Under the KEEP column, write down things you wish to continue, e.g., praying, journaling, or spending quality time with my children, etc. Under the START column, list things you would like to start, e.g., business plan, writing a book, exercising regularly, etc. Finally, under the STOP column note things that you want to stop, e.g., watching hours of television, social media marathons, eating fast food, etc. Often, your start and stop sections will be equal. This indicates that if you stop doing the things that are not purposeful, you would have more time for the things you must start. Use your start list as an action item list. When you fill compelled to do something from your stop list, chose from the start list instead. This will help you to maximize your time.

#MaximizingEachMoment

Decree: Lord, help me to maximize each moment. Let my management of time be responsible and intentional. I will stop wasting it and start making it count!

THE **PUSH**

Pray   **Plan**   **Reflect**

_____

_____

_____

_____

_____

_____

_____

_____

_____

_____

_____

_____

_____

_____

_____

_____

_____

_____

_____

_____

_____

_____

_____

_____

_____

_____

_____

_____

_____

Day 13 Processed for a Purpose
Jeremiah 1:5

Anything made goes through a process. Things that are made are processed based on the intended purpose or use. The materials chosen and even the testing it endures is related to the purpose it is being designed to fulfill. So, it is with us, many of the hurts, pains, and trials were not intended to break us, but to build us. Both the good and bad experiences of life help to equip us for our purpose. The pushing and pressing formed us for God's unique purpose. Your process may not be my process, but it was designed to make you fit for His use. Do not let the hurt, pain, or even the memories of your past deter you from pursuing you purpose. Every experience was intentional for the fulfillment of your purpose. The process didn't break you, it built you!

#ProcessedPurpose

Decree: I have a God given assignment. I was chosen and processed to fulfill it. My pain had a purpose. My process has produced a quality assured product!

THE **PUSH**

Pray	Plan	Reflect

Day 14 Mistakes
John 3:17

Mistakes are inevitable on your journey towards your purpose. In fact, mistakes are instrumental in assisting you with getting there. The Lord knew we would fall, fumble, stumble, make a mess, make bad choices, and make mistakes. Instead of talking about it and leaving us to die in our dirt, He made a way--a way out, a way through, and a way around. He will do whatever it takes to bring us back to Him. It is okay to spend time determining what led to the mishap. It is also wise to reflect to determine if you are caught in a cycle, allowing your emotions to lead or yearning for some form of fulfillment externally that must be met internally. However, being stuck and condemning yourself is not the answer. Wasting time harboring regret is also ineffective. Get back in there. Try again. Learn from your mistakes and allow God to restore you and recover what you may have lost. Pray for forgiveness and another opportunity. Instead of beating yourself up, be grateful for his endless mercies, unconditional love, and restoration power.

#MistakesGodAllowsRetakes

Decree: Lord, forgive me for any mistake I've made. I will learn the lesson and live in the new knowledge. Thank you for loving me beyond my mistakes. I will get back up again and finish my journey to my destiny.

THE **PUSH**

Pray	Plan	Reflect

_____

_____

_____

_____

_____

_____

_____

_____

_____

_____

_____

_____

_____

_____

_____

_____

_____

_____

_____

_____

_____

_____

_____

_____

_____

_____

_____

_____

Day 15 Let it Go!
Matthew 6:14-15

Try walking around all day with your fist clinched around an object. You will find that the object is likely to be fine, but you will experience pain and discomfort. It will also make it difficult to handle tasks put before you. This is true when we will not release those who have hurt us. Releasing them frees you to live and be open to obtain what God has for you. If your hands are full of pain, unforgiveness, and revenge you will block the very thing you were seeking in the first place…. LOVE. Don't let unforgiveness cause you to forfeit your promise.

#ForgivenessIsForMe

Decree: I will let go of bitterness, resentment, and hurt. I will forgive that I may be forgiven. I will not allow the inflicted pain of another to eat away at my future. The pain stops here, and I release forgiveness.

THE **PUSH**

Pray   **Plan**   **Reflect**

_____

_____

_____

_____

_____

_____

_____

_____

_____

_____

_____

_____

_____

_____

_____

_____

_____

_____

_____

_____

_____

_____

_____

_____

_____

_____

_____

_____

_____

_____

Day 16 When God Moves
Psalms 27:14

Sometimes God moves quickly! Other times, He seems to prolong the journey making the destination seem so far away. But it is in the waiting that He builds you for His purpose. The right process is what leads to a quality product. Don't rush it! It is already in motion. It's happening now. Each moment in the process is equipping you. Each prayer is sustaining you. Every dream is humbling you. Don't hate the process, it is what will make you strong enough to sit amongst the high and low and be consistent in character. Thank God for the process, while keeping the product in sight.

#PatienceInTheProcess

Decree: I will wait for direction from the Lord. I know that a delay is not a denial and a not now is not a never!

THE **PUSH**

Pray   **Plan**   **Reflect**

Day 17 The Vision
Genesis 6:13-18

Has God ever shown a vision to you? The vision is exciting. However, after the vision we receive direction that doesn't always make sense to us. Sometimes God's directions even come close to embarrassing. Noah had to build an ark for something he had never seen. The vision was great; his family would be saved. The method was odd, a flood would come where there had been no rain. Noah had to obey and trust God. He saved his family by doing so. In this season, God is looking for mature Christian disciples who can do what God requests, just because he requested it. Often, we desire the result, but don't understand God's methods to getting us there. We can become so engulfed in the idea of the destiny that we don't seek or allow God to direct the journey. The vision that God has given you, will bless you! Your obedience will get you there. There are bountiful, generational, and stored up blessings in your obedience to God's assignment and plan. Don't abort the mission because it does not look like the destiny.

#TrustGodsPlan

Decree: Lord I trust your vision and your plan. Order my steps. Guide my feet. Lead the way and I will follow. I will be obedient to the Lord's request and remain faithful to the journey.

THE **PUSH**

Pray   **Plan**   **Reflect**

Day 18 The Testimony
Revelations 12:11

As you pursue your purpose and even before you knew what your purpose was, God was developing your spiritual resume. Your spiritual resume is your testimony. Don't be afraid to embrace your testimony. It does not matter where you see yourself going or what your purpose is, you will come forth with a testimony. In public, I have had my heart broken, been humiliated, failed, experienced loss, and pain. In public, God has healed my heart, elevated me, restored, won battles giving me the credit, and paid me double for my pain. Don't hate your glory or your story. Celebrate your testimony and use it in your arena to draw others to Christ. Every happy ever after, started with a once upon a time.

#Testimony=SpiritualResume

Decree: I am an overcomer! I have won so many battles with the Lord on my side! I will tell of His goodness, mercy, and grace wherever I go! I've already won!

THE **PUSH**

Pray　　　　　　　　　　**Plan**　　　　　　　　　**Reflect**

_____

_____

_____

_____

_____

_____

_____

_____

_____

_____

_____

_____

_____

_____

_____

_____

_____

_____

_____

_____

_____

_____

_____

_____

_____

_____

THE **PUSH**

Day 19 Transition
Genesis 12:1, Acts 7:3 & Hebrews 11:8

When flying in a plane there is the takeoff, flight, and landing. Each possess some level of discomfort. The takeoff forces us back into our seats. Seat belts fastened we leave the ground (comfort) and take off into the air. Pushing against the air with such force, the plane shakes. The weight of the plane, passengers and baggage is now in the air. Once the plan reaches the desired altitude everything that appeared large, now looks small. We are now far away from where we started and there is no turning back. We do not elevate until we have arrived at our destination. We may have to taxi around waiting for our turn to arrive at our destiny. When given the go, the plane is lowered and the weight of everything that once seemed weightless is now lowered to the ground for a bumpy, body shifting, noisy landing. This was all necessary to transition from where we were to where we are going. So, it is with us! Transition can be difficult but being stuck in what is comfortable or average should be more difficult. Wasted potential is sinful and a life of regret leads to bitterness. Bind fear and procrastination and lose faith, power, strength, and determination. Fasten your seatbelt, pack light, and get a window seat. You're on your way to your destiny. The discomfort will seem minimal when you realize the magnitude of your destination. Greater is just beyond the turbulence!

#TravelingThroughTransition

Decree: I will get ready for my shift in location, position, and posture. I am ready to transition into my next phase of the journey. I'm ready!

THE **PUSH**

Pray	Plan	Reflect

Day 20 Goals
Habakkuk 2:2

Oftentimes, we reach a point of frustration because we have not accomplished our goals. Reevaluate your goals. Do you have too many? Does one conflict with another? Are your goals specific? Do they include timelines? Have you placed the date of completion on your calendar? Have you assessed your resources? Do you have what you need to accomplish your goal, i.e., time, money, capacity, information, and training, etc.? Change is a process not an event. Pick two clear goals to accomplish and once met, move on to another goal. Be sure to include what you will need to accomplish them. Also break the goal down into smaller steps with due dates for each step. Setting too many goals will leave them all unaccomplished or at best, done in an average fashion. It is better to focus on the quality of what you accomplish rather than the quantity.

#FocusedGoals

Decree: Lord, help me to set clear goals that will lead me to my appointed season and promise. Help me to formulate a clear vision that matches your vision for my life. I will walk in the spirit of excellence. Everything I put my hands to shall be blessed.

THE **PUSH**

Pray	Plan	Reflect

_____

_____

_____

_____

_____

_____

_____

_____

_____

_____

_____

_____

_____

_____

_____

_____

_____

_____

_____

_____

_____

_____

_____

_____

_____

_____

_____

_____

_____

_____

Day 21 Enough
2 Kings 4:1-6

When you have been called to a purpose greater than you, it can make you feel that you are not enough or inadequate. You may feel you are not educated enough, don't have enough resources or support, and you may even feel that your weaknesses will be exposed. The woman in 2 Kings 4:1-6 experienced the death of her husband. His death marked the end of her provision and left her in debt. When the prophet asked her what she had in her house, she noted that she only had a little oil. Her response indicates that what she possessed was not adequate for the job. She was told to borrow vessels from her neighbors (not a few), close the door on her and her children, and pour the oil into the vessels. This must have sounded unusual because she clearly didn't have enough oil for multiple vessels. She was still required to pour out. The widow was obedient and as she poured out God replaced what she poured supernaturally. She filled every vessel she collected. God would have filled whatever she collected.

The lesson is this, you may not feel you have enough, but God will replace what you pour out. In faith, pour out your little and watch God replace as you pour. In the end, the widow poured out so much oil there was enough for her to sell in order to rescue her sons from being taken, pay her debts, and live off the rest with her family. Her little was made much through her act of obedience and faith. She could have hung on to the little she had, but she would have never tapped into the sufficiency God had for her future and her family.

#WithGodIHaveEnough

Decree: My little is enough for God! I will pour out my gift. God is all sufficient and will provide what I need!

THE **PUSH**

Pray	Plan	Reflect

Day 22 Grace
Romans 8:1

We are far from perfect, unworthy of the tremendous blessings God has given. We may get frustrated with ourselves, inpatient, and at times choose our own way. However, no matter how far from his plan we drift, He always pulls us back in with such love and compassion. It is the love of Christ that draws us and His grace that keeps us. That is why we cannot spend our time beating ourselves up because of our mistakes and imperfections. As much as we strive to be like God we will fall short and when we do, we must get back up. Stay in the fight! Fight against self-pity and doubt. Fight against getting stuck in your mistake(s). Fight your way out of condemnation. When you make a mistake, repent, ask God for forgiveness, and forgive yourself.

#GraceToGetUpAgain

Decree: I will walk according to God's will for my life. I will do what I can to make wise choices and decisions! I will not wallow in wrong doing and/or sin. Lord, give me a heart of repentance when I fall short of your glory. Don't let me get stuck in condemnation. I am a conqueror and I am victorious.

THE **PUSH**

Pray   **Plan**   **Reflect**

_____

_____

_____

_____

_____

_____

_____

_____

_____

_____

_____

_____

_____

_____

_____

_____

_____

_____

_____

_____

_____

_____

_____

_____

_____

_____

_____

_____

_____

THE **PUSH**

Day 23 The Elevator Effect: Behind Closed Doors
Mark 16:6, Second Kings 4:4 & Matthew 25:10

Anything precious that grows and develops in nature usually does so beneath the surface, within dirt, rock, coal, or inside a shell. Consider plant roots, diamonds, gold, and pearls. They are pulled out, sprung up, or excavated. You can't always visibly see what lies beneath.

Riding on an elevator, I noticed something awesome. Before the elevator transitions up, the doors must be closed. In some cases, you can't see the transition occurring. You must believe by faith and feel yourself elevating.

Elevation and preparation rarely happen in the public eye. They happen behind closed doors. Your preparation happens when you are covered. If you wait the doors will open when you arrive at your destination/destiny. The ground will open for you as your roots push from beneath the surface and spring forth. How do I know;

- Jesus was buried before his resurrection (Mark 16:6)
- The certain woman in 2 Kings 4:4 had to shut the door to manifest the miracle
- The bridegroom came for the virgins who were ready, and they went in and the door was shut (Matt. 25:10).

Don't worry about who knows or believes in your process. God will expose the making of His masterpiece in due time. Shut the door on all the noise, distractions, and outside opinions. Allow God to cover you during your process. The most beautiful, valuable, priceless, rare, and authentic jewels are made this way. They are covered up, behind closed doors, beneath the surface, and found in places that look nothing like the beauty they produce. Your elevation will happen as soon as the doors of distraction are closed, and you get alone with God, behind closed doors.

THE **PUSH**

#BehindClosedDoors

Decree: Lord, help me to stay covered until You are ready to reveal me. Let the doors stay closed until I am elevated and arrive at your desired destination.

Pray   Plan   Reflect

_____

_____

_____

_____

_____

_____

_____

_____

_____

_____

_____

_____

_____

_____

_____

_____

_____

_____

_____

_____

_____

_____

_____

_____

_____

_____

_____

THE **PUSH**

Day 24 You Won't Find Me Where You Left Me
Mark 16:6 & Matthew 28:1-10

Those who crucified Jesus didn't know His destiny was one of resurrection and his crowning as King of Kings. In this text the people who knew Jesus intimately and were with Him before and/or during his crucifixion, go to his tomb looking for Him. After experiencing abandonment, mocking, and the torturous pain of crucifixion, He was buried, and a stone put before His grave. After three days of appearing to be dead, I am sure it looked like it was over and that He wasn't who He said He was. Mary and Mary Magdalene looked for Jesus in the place where they heard He would be instead of where He said he would be. Isn't it amazing how people who know you and love you don't always get you! Jesus spent time before His death teaching God's plan for His life and it included going to prepare a place for His people. However, Mary and Mary Magdalene still went to look for Jesus where He was left. This mirrors our lives now. People will always look for you where you use to be. They will look for you in your place of weakness, in your old position, your old residence, but we need to tell them, "I'm not where you left me!"

When they came back looking for Jesus, He was not there, He had risen. If we are to reign with Him, we must suffer with Him. We must experience the crucifixion, people attempting to bury us, throwing dirt, and pronouncing us dead. But, remember when they came back to look for Jesus, He wasn't where they left him. When those who hurt you, attempting to tear you down, and left you to endure the pain of their abandonment come looking for you again (they always do), don't be in the same place or condition in which they left you. You may have left me afraid, lonely, desperate, but I am no longer in that place. Don't look for me there. Refuse to be where they left you!

They should not find you there! Get up from that place. Move on! Get up! Go! Don't get stuck where they left you. Give yourself permission to resurrect with power. Your assignment is to resurrect, live, and leave the grave they placed you in. If they left you depressed, afraid, and desperate, be joyful, full of faith, and confident when they return.

We all have places of comfort, humiliation, and embarrassment. We can all identify with staying somewhere too long. The most powerful thing you can do when the enemy believes you're done, dead, and finished, is to get up and not be where he left you! In the end, the angel tells Mary and Mary Magdalene He is not here, He has risen, come see the place where He laid. He wasn't where people expected Him to be, instead He had fulfilled His assignment and did not look like what he had been through.

#IWontBeThere

Decree: Lord, I don't have to stay where I was placed. I have resurrection power through you Lord. I won't stay in the tomb my enemies prepared for me. I won't be where they left me!

THE **PUSH**

Pray   **Plan**   **Reflect**

THE **PUSH**

Day 25 Believe
Genesis 15:1-6

When the vision God gave you is so much bigger than your reality......only believe! Abram had no seed, but God called him to be the father of nations. Abram's situation looked impossible. It was so ridiculous that his wife laughed at the thought of producing a child. Real vision requires real faith! The vision God gives is usually so much bigger than you, that it causes you to almost laugh at the thought. Don't let your now, dictate your later. God has plans to do exactly what he showed you in your due season. God can give you what you don't have and multiply it! Abram is a witness to God's ability to take the impossible and make it possible.

#ONLYBelieve

Decree: I will not lose sight of the vision God has given me. Even when my situation and surroundings look contrary to the vision, I will believe by faith that it will come to pass. Lord help me to stay firm in my faith. Lord, I believe.

THE **PUSH**

Pray	Plan	Reflect

_____

_____

_____

_____

_____

_____

_____

_____

_____

_____

_____

_____

_____

_____

_____

_____

_____

_____

_____

_____

_____

_____

_____

_____

_____

_____

_____

_____

Day 26 See it!
Isaiah 43:19-21

Right now, God is doing a new thing! It's springing up, NOW! Springing up implies that it will pop up with force. Will you perceive it?

In the spring plants begin to bloom that were planted previously. We do not see them until they spring through the dirt and reveal a process that has been brewing for some time. Often, we do not see what is taking place at the root. God is working on some things underground/undercover. We may be introduced to it when it springs forth, but it was in the works long before its' reveal. There are things God is working on that you cannot see. He is getting to the root of you and growing you up. Can you perceive it before we see it? If you can perceive it and believe it by faith, you will BEHOLD it! Having vision does not mean you see it in the physical, it means you see it with your eyes of faith.

#MyFaithSeesIt

Decree: Lord, I see your hand on my life! I believe you are doing a work in me. It is a great work and will be revealed in time.

THE **PUSH**

Pray	Plan	Reflect

Day 27 Hope
Hebrews 11:1 & Romans 5:5

If you have ever been disappointed or let down, you may have experienced the need to preserve your heart. Efforts to do so include, not getting excited about things or expecting very little from life or people. Hebrews 11:1 says, "Faith is the substance of things hoped for...". Don't let go of your hope. You will have what you believe, and things will be done according to your faith. Romans 5:5 declares that "...hope maketh not ashamed...". Believe God! Trust that He declares great things for you. Your hope is safe if it's in God. So, get your hopes up knowing that God won't let you down.

#MyHopeIsBuiltOnGod

Decree: Lord help me to be hopeful! Help me to hold on to my hope.

THE **PUSH**

Pray	Plan	Reflect

THE **PUSH**

Day 28 Principle of Faith & Vision
Second Kings 2:8-15

Second Kings 2:8-15 tells of Elijah and Elisha. Elisha requests a double portion of Elijah's spirit. He asked for a hard thing. Elijah responded, "If you see me when I am taken from you, it shall be so for you". Elisha's request teaches us a few principles. 1) By faith ask for the hard thing you desire. 2) If you see it, you can have it. 3) When you support someone else's vision, God will bless you with your own. The relationship between these two made it possible for Elisha to receive what Elijah left behind. It also made it possible for Elisha to continue in the legacy.

#Principles

Decree: I see the invisible. I have vision. I am a vision supporter and a vision caster. I will seek a successor to continue my vision.

THE **PUSH**

Pray   **Plan**   **Reflect**

Day 29 The Company We Keep
Luke 1:36-41

Luke 1:36-41 tells of Mary and Elisabeth. After Mary has been in the presence of God and received the word of God spoken over her, she greets Elisabeth. Upon their greeting, the baby Elisabeth was pregnant with leaps in her womb. We can learn a lot from this encounter. 1) We must surround ourselves with people who have been in the presence of God. 2) The God in them will remind you of what's inside of you. 3) If you are pregnant with dreams and vision, guard your baby until it's time to push. Proverbs 13:20 tells us that, "he who walks with the wise grows wise, but a companion of fools suffers harm".

#InGoodCompany

Decree: I will be mindful of the company I keep. I will surround myself with those who are connected to God.

THE **PUSH**

Pray   **Plan**   **Reflect**

Day 30 Stay Connected
John 15:7

People won't expect an unplugged TV to have power or do what it was designed to do, but they will expect the power of God in their lives without being connected to him! Power outages are frustrating because they prevent us from accessing information, being entertained, and having the modern conveniences we have grown accustomed to. It is even more detrimental when the power outage is not one in the natural but the spiritual. When we disconnect from God we cannot gain information critical in our decision making and future. When we are not connected to God we find ourselves lacking joy and life seems meaningless. Being disconnected from God is inconvenient, because often life throws us situations that we cannot handle on our own and without Him life seems like a bully.

We must make a conscious effort to connect to God through prayer, fasting, and studying God's word. It is so easy to be distracted by life and all its' events that titter on crises. We must intentionally structure our day for time with our heavenly father. In His presence, we will gain insight into our day, gain clarity, and find all that we seek. Plan to connect with God. Once connected, stay connected.

#PowerSource #LifeLine #NoOutages

Decree: Lord, I desire to get connected and remain connected to you. Lord let me be found in your presence daily and let me find peace, joy, and direction in your presence.

THE **PUSH**

Pray   **Plan**   **Reflect**

_____

_____

_____

_____

_____

_____

_____

_____

_____

_____

_____

_____

_____

_____

_____

_____

_____

_____

_____

_____

_____

_____

_____

_____

_____

_____

THE **PUSH**

Day 31 Breaking Cycles
Deuteronomy 1:6

"Deuteronomy 1:6- You have stayed long enough at this mountain."

This is the season of transition in your life and in the body of Christ. Recognize it! Trust that God is directing your path and be obedient to His instructions. Do not spend 40 years doing what should only take 11 days. We must stop going in circles and venture out into the promise. Cycles are repeated behaviors that create a predictable pattern in our lives. When we continue to handle our problems the same way, we risk being trapped in a cycle. There is good news; you can break the cycles. I must warn you! Breaking a cycle is uncomfortable. You may have become so physically, emotionally, and even spiritually accustomed to the cycle that breaking out of it feels scary. When exiting a cycle, you are walking into unchartered territory; places you've never been, things you may not have seen. Don't let your fear or lack of knowledge cause you to jump back into the familiar. Instead, embrace the newness as an indication of a new you with new possibility. Identify the cycles in your life and change the patterns.

#CycleBreaker #MovingForward

Decree: I will not repeat the mistakes of my past. I am a new creature. I am creating a new future that is full of hope and success. The familiar is an enemy to my future so I will embrace the newness that I am approaching. I am venturing into new territory and I will possess it!

THE **PUSH**

Pray	Plan	Reflect

Day 32 God MAKES a Way!
Exodus 14:21-22

God makes ways for us when there seems to be no way! When we find ourselves between a rock and a hard place, we must stretch out our faith as Moses stretched out his hand. Moses (The Leader) led his people to a place where impossibility (Red Sea) was on one side and the enemy was on the other! When you are in the middle of (you insert whatever you wish here) believe God will make a way. He can make the impossible, possible when we believe. See your sea parting. Know that this is a divine set up for God to show up. He often gives our enemy front row seats to see His master plan unfold. God will perform a miracle to fulfill His word. Go in faith and watch God make a way, where there was no way.

#HeIsMakingAWay

Decree: God already has a plan that I may not see. I will be obedient to his commands. I expect a miracle. I expect God to make a way out of my situation. I see my sea parting.

THE **PUSH**

Pray   **Plan**   **Reflect**

_____

_____

_____

_____

_____

_____

_____

_____

_____

_____

_____

_____

_____

_____

_____

_____

_____

_____

_____

_____

_____

_____

_____

_____

_____

_____

_____

_____

Day 33 Favor Over Fear
Genesis 39:21 & Proverbs 8:35

Lord remind me of your favor on my life despite where I am and what surrounds me. There is no need to be frustrated or live in fear when you have God's favor.

Favor is not placed on you because you are so wonderful, intelligent, or wise. Favor is a result of being connected and loved by our Heavenly Father. It is not a tool of separation, to distinguish one Christian from another but rather a manifestation of God's love, grace, and kindness towards us. We have favor over our lives, but let's not be foolish. Favor rest and remains on those who never forget we are still not worthy.

#Favor #FavorOverFear

Decree: I have favor over my life. I can trust that God favors me. I am thankful for His favor. I believe His favor is opening and closing doors for me. I take no credit for God's work in my life. I believe His favor is for my good and for His glory.

THE **PUSH**

Pray   **Plan**   **Reflect**

THE **PUSH**

Day 34 Transition
Genesis 19:26, Philippians 3:14 & Psalms 121:1

Are you trying to transition to the next level? Attempting to soar? Let me give you a word of advice, "Don't look down!" Don't look at where you came from (Lot's wife). Looking back prevents forward progression. Why look in a direction you do not wish to go? Back is not an option. Don't let the elevation alter your oxygen levels causing it to go to your head. When God begins to take you to higher heights it means more exposure. Don't let the glory of it all go to your head. Remember, it is God's doing and not your own. Stay humble! Don't look down on others. Don't allow the enemy to cause you to forget that not everyone has your support system, parents, relationships, or background. Your elevation is not just about you. It is about leading someone else through the glass ceilings of life. Your success is more rewarding when you take someone with you. Look to the hills and remember where your help came and comes from (Psalms 121:1). Give Him glory in all things. Use every moment of triumph to make the name of Jesus great. Be a witness to His great faithfulness!

#DontLookDown

Decree: I am full of faith, humble, and a mentor. The glory belongs to God and I am honored to be chosen to serve.

THE **PUSH**

Pray	Plan	Reflect

_____

_____

_____

_____

_____

_____

_____

_____

_____

_____

_____

_____

_____

_____

_____

_____

_____

_____

_____

_____

_____

_____

_____

_____

_____

_____

_____

_____

_____

_____

Day 35 Obstacles
Numbers 13:30

Pray, Lord give me the determination to get everything you have for me and not give up until I have it!

Caleb, after seeing the giants in the land promised to his people, STILL declared, "We are well able to overcome it". Whatever giant is between you and your promise, it is there for you to overcome it! The giants were assigned to your life for a purpose. Don't be distracted by the size of your situation, how the same giant has taken out others, or the fear of failure. The bigger the giant the greater the testimony. It's your giant. Get over it! Stare at it and declare, I am well able to get over this! You are an overcomer. If the Lord did not believe you could conquer it, He would not have assigned it to you. Whatever is standing before your promise is not meant to deter you from fulfilling God's ordained destiny in your life. The giant is a test of your faith. Pass the test. Your belief about the giants and how you see them determines if generations behind you will live in your promise or be stuck in mediocrity. Develop a strategy that uses the size of your obstacle to your advantage. Be creative in your approach to the situation. Ask God to help you see the giant differently. You, indeed, are well able to overcome it!

#BigGiantBiggerGod

Decree: I am well able to overcome every challenge assigned to my life! God has placed everything in me that I need to destroy giants! I will walk the next generation into the promise! My promise matters! God is bigger than every giant! God is for me and will help me with the obstacles of life!

THE **PUSH**

Pray	Plan	Reflect

_____

_____

_____

_____

_____

_____

_____

_____

_____

_____

_____

_____

_____

_____

_____

_____

_____

_____

_____

_____

_____

_____

_____

_____

_____

_____

_____

_____

_____

Day 36 The Heart
Psalms 51:10-12

The heart is a tricky thing to handle. It is essential that we check its condition daily. Checking the heart's condition ensure that we do not become bitter, hard, or wicked. Often, we work to alter our words, thoughts, and actions, without regard for the heart they come from. The heart is the central controlling force to many of the issues of life. The condition of our heart determines what flows from our spirit. The condition of our heart can change quickly. That is why we must take it to be examined daily. We may think we know all the issues of our heart, but why not take it to the one who knows its complexity and layers. Ask God to examine your heart. Ask Him to remove the debris of past hurt and the bitterness that makes it hard to give and receive love. You know it's time. The barriers you have placed around your heart make you feel protected but have blocked you from receiving the love of others and God. Pray this simple prayer, "Create in me a clean heart, O God: and renew a right spirit within me. Cast me not away from thy presence and take not thy Holy Spirit from me. Restore unto me the joy of thy salvation and uphold me with thy free spirit." (Psalms 51:10-12).

#CleanHeart

Decree: My heart is clean, pliable, and full of love. I release anything that prevents me from receiving love. Love flows through me.

THE **PUSH**

Pray	Plan	Reflect

Day 37 Love
John 15:13

"Greater love hath no man than this, that a man lay down his life for his friends" (John 15:13). Today I stand in awe of God's love for you and me! Understanding His greatness and power, it still brings tears to my eyes that He considers us friends. I am working to make this friendship a little less one sided by staying in touch with Him; getting to know more about Him; and being available when He needs me! If we are going to achieve our purpose, we need direction constantly. We must stay connected to God through prayer. We must communicate. Can you imagine having a friend that never calls, texts, or visits? Over time, the friendship will suffer, and you will know less about their current life. We owe God our time. It takes effort to sustain this relationship. Don't lose your connection! In addition to staying connected, we should want to know more about Him. We learn about Him through His word and through experiences applying His word. There is always more to learn about God. Be sure that you do not spend time telling Him all about you, and never listen or take time to learn about Him. I want to know Him in the depths of my soul. If we are going to be friends, we must be available. Think about it. Friends are there. They are present at the most critical times of your life. Friends are not just present when things are good, they also provide support when things are bad. Friendship is not based on convenience but, a mutual love for one another. I know He's been our friend. The question is, how good of a friend have we been?

#RealFriends

Decree: I am a friend of God. I am committed to staying connected, knowing more about Him, and being in His presence. I am grateful that He calls me friend.

THE **PUSH**

Pray	Plan	Reflect

Day 38 BE YOU
Psalms 139:14

It is okay to look fabulous but, it is better to be fabulous. Otherwise it is just a disguise, a knockoff, or an image. Misrepresenting yourself leads to temporary relationships, flawed character, and exhaustion from trying to hold on to it all. When you are not authentic, people do not get a chance to love you. They merely love your representative. This prevents you from feeling or receiving authentic love in return.

Identity theft is illegal. Take the chance and expose who you really are, people will either love you or hate you, but either way, at least it will be genuine. Embrace the uniqueness that is you! Heels, sneakers, weave, natural, makeup, no makeup, these things don't make you who you are. If you determine your value based on things, you will be worth only the amount of those things. Your purpose requires an authentic you. Your destiny belongs to the real you! God wants every area that is not genuine to be uncovered and dealt with through His precious love for you. He is willing to heal the broken and insecure areas. Isn't that what keeps you from loving the real you? Don't worry about who may not like the parts of you that are yet to be developed and the parts that still need God's work. The very thing you feel insecure about is what makes you unique and relatable. In business who you are is a part of your brand, it is what makes your product and service uniquely yours. Self-work is continuous. It is okay to be uniquely you in the moment, knowing that who I am today will not be who I am tomorrow. The real you is priceless! Be uniquely you!

#LovingMeInTheMoment

Decree: I am fearfully and wonderfully made. My uniqueness is opening doors for me! The more I am me, the closer I am to God's original design. My destiny requires that I show up authentic! I love me now and later!

THE **PUSH**

Pray   **Plan**   **Reflect**

Day 39 Recognizing a Wolf
Matthew 7:15

Matthew 7:15 cautions us to beware of false prophets, which come to you in sheep's clothing, but inwardly they are raving wolves. Matthew 10:16 informs us that we are sent as sheep amid wolves. One challenge you will face on the road to your purpose is determining who should be in your circle of influence. People can become distractions to your purpose. To make consistent progress towards your purpose you need the wisdom to know the difference between sheep and wolves prior to them revealing themselves. If wolves can disguise themselves as sheep, how do you spot a wolf? By their fruit and/or behavior. Wolves are diggers by nature. They will dig for information in your past looking for something they can use. Check around you. Are you surrounded by people who know all your problems and secrets, but you know nothing about them? Oftentimes, this is wrapped in a pretty package of concern and the desire to help you. Beware, not everybody who arrives in your dark season has good intentions.

Pray about connecting to new people and what information to share. Practice temperance! Don't get so excited about finally having support that you open yourself up to hurt and abuse. Pray for Godly connections with a sincere heart towards you. Pray for discernment. Wolves eat and regurgitate for their pups. Disgusting right? They take your business in and then give it out to their crew or pack. Their connection with you makes them relevant to others. These people are dangerous. The people who help you should always have a dream of their own and walk in their own purpose even if they are assigned to assist you with yours. A wolf's bite is twice as powerful as a dog's bite. Their mouths hurt others. Don't wait for their mouths to hurt you. If they are hurtful to others, it is only a matter of time before that same poison hits you. Don't get bit! Stay watchful. You can never be so busy, you avoid discerning a sheep from a wolf. Examine your circle, are they sheep or wolves?

THE **PUSH**

#SheepVsWolf

Decree: I have discernment. I have the power to see who is for me and who is against me. My eyes are open. I use wisdom to make Godly connections.

THE PUSH

Pray   **Plan**   **Reflect**

Day 40 It is not Over!
Matthew 9:18-28

Matthew 9:18-28 tells of a ruler's daughter who was dead. The ruler believed that Jesus could bring his daughter back to life. In verse 24, Jesus says, "give place for the maid is not dead, but sleepeth". Are there things in your life you have given up on because it looked dead? Maybe it was a business you started that didn't work out, your marriage, relationships, or your last pursuit of your purpose. Sometimes what appears to be dead is simply lying dormant. Many of us have cried over, mourned, and eulogized areas of our lives that were not dead. Reevaluate these areas, perhaps these areas are not dead, but sleep. Death and sleep looks similar. While we are sleep there is still breath in our bodies, we are not cold, and we can think and reason. Maybe we need to take a minute to breathe, soften our hearts, and consider a strategy for reawakening what we thought lacked potential or would never work. Look again! This time with your spiritual eyes of hope. You may find that you gave up too quick on something that still had life in it. Consider this your alarm clock! Whatever had been sleep in your life must wake up! There is still hope, if YOU can see it breathing.

#ISeeItBreathing

Decree: I am reevaluating my life. I'm looking for areas that I may need to revisit and conquer. My spiritual eyes are open. I am beyond optimistic, I'm hopeful. I can see it breathing.

THE **PUSH**

Pray   **Plan**   **Reflect**

_____

_____

_____

_____

_____

_____

_____

_____

_____

_____

_____

_____

_____

_____

_____

_____

_____

_____

_____

_____

_____

_____

_____

_____

_____

_____

_____

_____

_____

_____

Day 41 Answer the Call
First Thessalonians 5:24

"Faithful is he that calleth you, who also will do it". (I Thessalonians 5:24) God often calls us to things we don't feel equipped enough to walk into. We find ourselves questioning why God called US. Why me? If you are anything like me, you even attempt to give God a list of those you believe are better suited for the job. I have also found that God calls us higher and deeper at the same time. He calls us to places we have never been, to give us the relationship with him that we have never had. God's call comes with discomfort and a need to trust Him. The call takes the type of trust that depends solely on the voice of God, His word and wise counsel. The call often feels lonely, but God is there. To answer God's call takes a great deal of faith. Faith that God can use YOU to accomplish His assignment in the Earth. Yes, you! You with your insecurities, procrastination, issues, and short comings. I know you would like to be perfect first, but that just won't happen.

Even with all the reasons you want to say no, say yes to the call of God. Answer the call. It is amazing the amount of people who run from the Call. Many because they feel insecure, unworthy, and incompetent when it comes to ministry or marketplace. The truth of the matter is that while we must live a life of integrity and holiness, we will never be deserving or reach perfection. Let your personal goals be simple. 1) Stay connected to God through relationship. 2) Push to be better, daily. 3) Repent when you miss it. The One who called you, will do the work! Trust Him not your ability! The question being are you available to be used? Answer the call. Someone needs what you have.

#GodCalledIAnswered

THE **PUSH**

Decree: I am called by God to do mighty works through Him! Connected to Him, there is nothing impossible for me! I can do all things through Christ that strengthens me! Today I say yes to the will of God for my life.

THE **PUSH**

Pray   **Plan**   **Reflect**

_____

_____

_____

_____

_____

_____

_____

_____

_____

_____

_____

_____

_____

_____

_____

_____

_____

_____

_____

_____

_____

_____

_____

_____

_____

_____

_____

_____

_____

_____

THE **PUSH**

Day 42 Pardon the Interruption
Luke 7:36-39

Luke 7:36-39 tells of a woman who is described as a sinner. She finds out Jesus is at a Pharisee's house eating and she interrupts the dinner to give Jesus all she had (oil from an alabaster box). I am sure the polite thing to do would have been to ask Jesus to step out to speak with Him. Or, maybe she should have waited until He was done. This woman didn't care who was around. She wasn't embarrassed, ashamed, or concerned with what people would think. She showed up desperate for the attention of the only one who mattered in that moment. She wanted Jesus. Not only did she know who she was coming to see, she knew exactly what she was planning to do. She came to give Him the best that she had to offer. She came with expensive oil from her alabaster box.

Let's go to God knowing his capability to free us, change us, and deliver us. Let us go desperate and with the best that we have to offer. This woman sets an example of how to approach Jesus. I am so glad we serve a God who; 1) responds to worship, 2) does not see us the way others do, and 3) forgives us in the face of doubters. Look at who is in your room. The room of life. Who is witnessing your encounters with God, your desperation, and you giving of the best you have. This woman was a sinner in the room with Jesus and a Pharisee. A Pharisee represents those who believe they do not have a need for Jesus because they live so perfect. Pharisees also look down on others who are not in their circle. Examine your circumstances. Do you know Jesus? Are there a few Pharisee around you? If you are a sinner, you are in the right position to be blessed. He STILL forgives, saves, and washes. Thank the Lord!

#MeAndAPharisee

THE **PUSH**

Decree: I'm desperate for God's presence! I'm bring the best that I have to offer God. I'm not concerned with who is watching. My only concern is Jesus. I'm here to worship!

Pray   **Plan**   **Reflect**

_____

_____

_____

_____

_____

_____

_____

_____

_____

_____

_____

_____

_____

_____

_____

_____

_____

_____

_____

_____

_____

_____

_____

_____

_____

_____

_____

_____

THE **PUSH**

Day 43 Soul Prosperity
Third John 1:2

Third John 1:2, "Beloved, I wish above all things that thou mayest prosper and be in health, even as thy soul prospereth". God wants us to have a balanced life, where our soul's prosperity dictates your entire life's level of prosperity. It does us no good to prosper financially if our souls end up in hell or our health won't allow us to enjoy it. The soul must come first in our list of priorities. Prospering the soul takes prayer, fasting, and consistent study of the word of God. For your soul to prosper we must apply what we receive from prayer, fasting, and the word of God. Notice the texts says prospereth, suggesting that does not just happen once but it is continuous. When your soul prospers, your finances prosper, your relationships prosper, etc... This also informs us that God desires that we be in good health. Are you healthy enough to pursue what God has for you? Can the weight of the anointing rest on your shoulders without your heart collapsing under the pressure? We are not just spirit, we are physical. We must create time to prosper in our soul/spirit, health, and finances. Today seek to prosper as your soul prospers.

#IShallPropser

Decree: I am prospering in every area of my life. I will invest time, energy, and effort in my soul. My soul is prospering! My health is prospering! My finances are prospering! My life is whole.

THE **PUSH**

Pray   **Plan**   **Reflect**

_____

_____

_____

_____

_____

_____

_____

_____

_____

_____

_____

_____

_____

_____

_____

_____

_____

_____

_____

_____

_____

_____

_____

_____

_____

_____

_____

_____

_____

_____

Day 44 King's Kid
Second Samuel 9:1-13

Second Samuel 9:1-13 tells of Mephibosheth who was royalty (son of Jonathan, grandson of King Saul). Mephibosheth was crippled. He was immobile or unable to walk. He was stuck just like many of us. The interesting thing is that Mephibosheth did not get stuck because he did something wrong. Somebody dropped Mephibosheth when he was only five years old (Second Samuel 4:4). Can you imagine spending the rest of your life stuck because of someone else's mistake? Can you imagine being royal, a member of the king's family but cannot move? Some of us don't have to imagine it. Some of us have been stuck for years because someone dropped us. Being dropped can result in being stuck- in pain, bitterness, fear of rejection, abandonment issues, low self-esteem, fear of failure, and so many other silent, but powerful results.

We are the children of the king, yet we forget the authority that comes with this relationship. We do not have to live stuck; being stuck is more than a place, it is a posture and position. Mephibosheth did not have to stop living and stop thriving just because one part of him was no longer capable of functioning as expected. There is good news, there is life after being dropped. Despite his condition, Mephibosheth ended up at the king's table because of who his father was. Remember, you may feel stuck, but you are the child of the King and your place is set at the table and in the palace. You belong there! It is your inheritance. You are an heir. I don't care how bad your condition is or what you have been through, if you are a child of God, you have rights and privileges!! Your place is in the palace. Make the switch from being a victim to a victor. Your daddy is the King!

#Royalty

THE **PUSH**

Decree: I am the son/daughter of a king. I am progressing forward! My past does not define me, my father does! I belong where God has placed me.

THE **PUSH**

Pray   **Plan**   **Reflect**

Day 45 Make It Personal
Hebrews 11:6

Get a PERSONAL relationship with God; not just a church, a doctrine, a relationship with the Pastor and First Lady, ushers, ministers, or another clergy. Get to know Jesus. It seems in this time, people try hard to connect with people, things, organizations, and networks but do not put forth greater or even equal effort to develop a relationship with Christ. We must love those who serve with us, but they should not be the priority. Serve Christ first. Serving God requires alone time with Him, seeking His face, and demonstrating your love for Him through a lifestyle of worship. This will not just happen, you must make it happen. Alone time with God should be a part of your day if you want to walk in your purpose. Cry out to God for direction and spend time in silence to hear His whisper. Worship God, not just in the waving of your hands, but in an attitude of gratitude and thanksgiving. We must seek God. He will lead you into your destined purpose for your life.

#ServeGod

Decree: I yearn for God! I thank you God for all things. My direction is found in you.

THE **PUSH**

Pray	Plan	Reflect

Day 46 Heart Check
Psalms 139:23-24

Today pray Psalms 139:23-24 "search me, O God, and know my heart: try me, and know my thoughts. And see if there be any wicked way in me and lead me in the way everlasting."

We must constantly ask God to evaluate us. We should also conduct self-reflections, quality evaluations, and/ checkups. In attempts to keep our hearts right, we must ask God to 1) **search me** because only the Maker knows the intended purpose of His creation. When God searches, He looks for the ingredients it takes to make what He intended us to be. He looks for integrity, character, and our motives. God knows how to look for what needs to be fixed or improved. He does this not to hurt our feelings, but to get us to our expected, predestined place. 2) **Know my heart.** The heart can become bitter and bruised. We can live in denial of what is truly in our hearts. The heart can also be misunderstood as our mouths and actions speak for our hearts. Sometimes our hearts are in the right place, but we lack the wisdom need to govern our hearts. Given the dynamic intricacies of the heart, we need God to know our hearts, so He can repair, cleanse, and fill us. 3) **Try me.** If it is worth having, it's been tested. We should all shout, "Lord try me, before you use me". We often have misconceptions concerning trials and tribulations. The assumption is that we have done something wrong and the trial is our punishment. These things are not sent to break us, but to build us. Trials draw out our character and strength. Tribulations results in making us resilient. 4) **Know my thoughts.** Our thoughts can roam. If left unchecked our thoughts can run away from us, our imaginations can run wild, and we can think ourselves into despair or destiny. Thoughts become actions. Repeated actions become habits. We must ask God to know our thoughts and reveal those that don't align with His thoughts. Finally, we need God to, 5) lead us in the way everlasting. It is essential that our ways please God and result in us having everlasting life.

THE **PUSH**

#ExaminationTime

Decree: Lord, examine me! Know my heart Lord. Try me and remove anything that is preventing me from being who you called me to be. Lord, know my thoughts and mute the noise so I can hear you!

THE **PUSH**

Pray   **Plan**   **Reflect**

_____

_____

_____

_____

_____

_____

_____

_____

_____

_____

_____

_____

_____

_____

_____

_____

_____

_____

_____

_____

_____

_____

_____

_____

_____

_____

_____

_____

THE **PUSH**

Day 47 The Fight
First Corinthians 9:26-27

First Corinthians 9:26-27, Paul writes to the church of Corinth reminding them to run the race like someone is running against them. He also says that he doesn't fight like he is fighting the air. That is because we have a real enemy that fights back. Someone can look great while shadow boxing or running alone, but when introduced to an opponent, fall apart. Mike Tyson said something profound, "everyone has a plan, until they get hit". Don't wait to get a plan after life hits you. We are in the fight for our lives. Our plan must include offense and defense. We cannot just fight we must also build. We cannot just spend, we must also save. We must talk and listen. Our plan must always include the offensive work that must be accomplished and the defensive prevention to avoid the pitfalls in life. Rainy days are guaranteed, be prepared for them.

On the road to accomplishing your dreams and living your purpose, the road will not always be easy. However, you can buy the right shoes, workout to build your stamina, stay in prayer, and keep God's word before you. When those times come the road is made easier because of proper preparation. The road is difficult to navigate when you must gather what you need on the way to where you are going. The road is too stony, the hill too high, the winds too fierce, and the voices are too loud to get ready in the mist. Build your spirit man up now! You will need everything you are learning in your now, for your next. What appears to be trouble now is only a training ground. Get a consistent prayer life and bible study time. The fight is real. We don't war against flesh and blood; our fight must be spiritual. The word still works and fasting still works. When the enemy comes in like a flood, lift a standard, not a fist. What will you do with your standing eight count? God will allow you time to get ready, get your legs back under you, and your mind focused. It's training day!

THE **PUSH**

It is also important not to judge a person's strength by what we view outside of the ring. The perspective of the ring on the outside appears to yield great advice. It's easy to tell someone else to punch, keep their arms up, and stay in the fight when you are not the one getting hit. We should be glad that Jesus is in our corner, fixing the cuts, and encouraging us to continue the fight. Victory is in the endurance and the battle has already been won.

#TheFightIsFixed

Decree: Lord, help me to prepare for what is ahead! My hands are at work building and fighting. I am willing to train hard to have what belongs to me. Victory belongs to me because of You!

THE **PUSH**

Pray   **Plan**   **Reflect**

_____

_____

_____

_____

_____

_____

_____

_____

_____

_____

_____

_____

_____

_____

_____

_____

_____

_____

_____

_____

_____

_____

_____

_____

_____

_____

_____

_____

_____

_____

Day 48 Faith Over Fear
Joshua 1:9, 11:6, Jeremiah 1:8 & Deuteronomy 31:6

Fear is often the obstacle that prevents many people from accomplishing their dreams. Don't let it! We can sometimes be afraid of failure or even success. God tells us in His word that we don't need to be afraid. Joshua 1:9, 11:6, Jeremiah 1:8, and Deuteronomy 31:6 tells us that we should not be afraid because He is with us, and 2) He can and will deliver us. He cannot fail. What are you afraid of? God's got it! If He told you to go, GO! You will likely feel some sense of inadequacy. You are not intended to know it all, have all the answers, and be perfect in your execution. God desires that we have faith and trust in Him. Trust Him and embrace the challenges that are sent to build your faith.

#FaithOverFear

Decree: I trust God with every area of my life. I can count on Him, when I cannot count on me. With God I can accomplish anything. I choose faith over fear.

THE PUSH

Pray   **Plan**   **Reflect**

Day 49 Life.... Speak Life
Proverbs 18:21

Death and life are in the power of the tongue. Life is the capacity to grow and reproduce. Death is the end of life or the end of growth and reproduction. We have the power, by faith, to speak life into our situation or speak death. It is a choice. If you feel you are not growing or being productive, examine what you say. An apple tree produces apples. Those apples contain a seed to produce more apples. The words we speak produce a seed that is planted. Those seeds/words then grow and produce more of what we say. What are you saying about you? Your situation? Your children? Your money? Your family? Life will be what you call it! Start now. Command four positive things about your life and do not take them back. Declare positive things over yourself, your children, and for others. Stay positive even when it looks negative. Do not lose hope or focus. It will not always be easy but speak life in faith! Begin to declare, I will be a blessing. I will move closer to my destiny. I will let go of the past, and I will have unquenchable joy. Amen.

#MyMouthBirthsMyManifestation

Decree: My life is rich and bountiful. I exude joy and hope. I see things working for me. My children are blessed and favored by God. My life is moving in the right direction. My family is God-led. I am wealthy in every area of my life.

THE **PUSH**

Pray   **Plan**   **Reflect**

THE **PUSH**

Day 50 Transformation
Romans 12:2 & Proverbs 23:7

Romans 12:2 reminds us that transformation occurs through the renewing of our minds. Think yourself into a better situation. See with your mind's eye a new joy in your life. Life is what you think it and call it! Yesterday I asked, what are you talking about? Today, we must search our thoughts. What are you thinking about? Do you take time to renew your mind? Do you think about, what you think about? It takes prayer to renew your mind; to release unwanted thoughts; and the word of God to replace those thoughts. God has specific thoughts concerning you and your life in His word. If our thoughts do not line up with what God says concerning us, we must get renewed. Consider your thoughts. Jot down a few thoughts that are not Godly. Find a scripture that counteracts and tells the truth about who and what you are in the kingdom. If your thought is, "I'm unattractive, nobody likes me." Consider Psalms 139:14, "I praise you because I am fearfully and wonderfully made". Replace your old thought with John 15:15, "God calls me friend". Proverbs 23:7 declares that we will be what we think about. Today guard your thoughts. Think on the good. Choose not to complain and believe today will be a great day. This will be a magnificent day. Do you agree?

#Mind+Mouth=Manifestation

Decree: I control my thoughts through God. I think on the word of God. God says I can, I can. God says I'm blessed, I'm blessed. My mind is clear, positive, and renewed.

THE PUSH

Pray	Plan	Reflect

Day 51 Press Forward
Philippians 3:13

In Philippians 3:13, Paul writes about the power of forgetting what is behind and reaching forward. Many times, we only do one part of the process. We forget but fail to reach or reach but fail to forget. It is not enough to let go and not reach beyond your current situation. For us to come out of the past, we must move forward into our glorious future. The past can hold us in bondage from our future. We must press! Press past the pain, negative thoughts, and doubts about tomorrow. Ask yourself if your beliefs about you are connected to what use to be true. Sometimes change has come and we are so busy reminding ourselves of yesterday, we cannot receive the beauty in our tomorrow that awaits. Our past can feel like a bungee cord springing us back every time we go forward. At times it is a slight tug and at other times, it is a full out war against your forward progression. Fight forward! Forge ahead. Ask God to remove anything from your past that prevents you from becoming everything you need to be to enjoy your future. Then focus on forward. What else Has he given you to do? What is in sight but not in your grasp? Reach for it! Break the cord.

#FightForward

Decree: My past is behind me and I leave it there. I am focused on forward! I see my future and I am pressing towards it with force, faith, and aggression.

THE **PUSH**

Pray   **Plan**   **Reflect**

Day 52 Believe God Loves YOU
Romans 8:35-39

It is easy for us to notice the good in others and be able to tell them that Christ loves them. Oftentimes the struggle is in knowing your own mess, mistakes, setbacks, failures, shortcomings, and doubts, but believe for yourself. It becomes difficult to believe that God loves you and can use you in the state you are in. Do not allow condemnation to block you from achieving your purpose. Perfection is not a prerequisite for your use. Romans 8:35-39 declares that there is nothing that can separate us from the love of God. Included in the nothing is YOU and me. We cannot separate ourselves from Christ's love. There is no need to wait until you are perfect to do what God has required of you. We should pursue holiness with the understanding that our shortcomings do separate us from the love of God. He does not stop loving us with every mistake. His love does not dwindle after every mishap. He is not fickle like people. God loves us beyond the shallow love we have experienced with so called friends and family. His love is unconditional and transcends us. Believe in God's love for YOU. Receive his love for you! Today let's thank Him for looking beyond our faults and loving us when we could not even stand ourselves. Let's thank Him for loving us when we didn't know how to love Him. There is no greater love, than that of our Lord Jesus Christ. It is often incomprehensible, but it is always real.

#HeLovesMe

Decree: God loves me! I receive His love for me! I break the barriers that have blocked me from resting in His love.

THE **PUSH**

Pray   **Plan**   **Reflect**

Day 53 Ordered Steps
Psalms 37:23-24

Psalms 37: 23-24 declares that "the steps of a good man are ordered...". I thank God that He has a plan for our lives. He has a sequence/order established to get us to our destiny. We often only see from our limited perspective and then determine what the next steps should be, but God will create a step or reveal a step we didn't see, to get us in the right direction. God orders our steps! How awesome is it that our God does not simply walk with us or point us in the right direction? He orders every single step we take. He has a master plan and a sequence of events that are necessary for His expected outcome. Your steps are not random, scattered, or guesswork to God. His work is within every step of your life. If you feel that you are walking in circles, change your navigation system and allow God to order your steps. Use caution! Do not allow money, competition, or fame to order your steps. These things can send you down a road that is not prepared for you. Chasing money, competing with people, or attempting to gain popularity are never reasons to choose a path. When these things seek to deter you from God's plan, resist. Following God may bring wealth, reward, and enlarged territories, but our desire should be kingdom building. Let God order your steps as Lord of your life.

#MyNextStepIsMyBestStep

Decree: My steps are order by God. My desire is God's path for my life. Every step I take matters.

THE **PUSH**

Pray	Plan	Reflect

Day 54 Support for the Vision
Genesis Chapters 6 & 7

The lack of support should NEVER impede your progress. Stop waiting for people to get on board and just build the boat. The vision was given to you, not them. They cannot see it, but once they do, they will jump on board. Noah built the ark! He didn't talk about building the ark. Lives were depending on him to do what was needed to be done, and they did not even know they needed his vision. God gave Noah the provision and resources followed by the need for them. Noah prepared for the unseen by building the ark before it rained. God will ask us to prepare for what is to come even when we do not understand what is coming. If Noah procrastinated, waited, or did not obey; his entire family would have drowned! Get ready! Build your dream and vision! The rain will surely come!

#DoItAlone

Decree: My vision is necessary to the kingdom. Even when others don't see it, help me remain focused on my vision! The vision God has given me will meet needs that are not seen yet.

THE **PUSH**

Pray   **Plan**   **Reflect**

_____

_____

_____

_____

_____

_____

_____

_____

_____

_____

_____

_____

_____

_____

_____

_____

_____

_____

_____

_____

_____

_____

_____

_____

_____

_____

_____

_____

_____

_____

_____

_____

117

THE **PUSH**

Day 55 Wait? God's Timing
Psalms 27:14, 37:34 & Habakkuk 2:3

WAIT! Psalms 27:14, 37:34, and Habakkuk 2:3 point out the need to wait! Waiting is not always easy, but it is necessary. In the process of waiting, there are several things that prepare you for the upcoming blessing. In waiting, patience, faith, and knowledge are gained. Getting a vision is great, but vision is for an appointed time. Be sure to not seek only vision and provision, but timing. Timing does matter! If you move too late you will miss the appointed time. Seek God for HIS timing! The wait is not designed to make you bitter, it is to make you better. God will do great work in you during the waiting. What time is it? What season is it in your life? Is it your season to move or wait? In education, wait time gives the learner a chance to gather their thoughts and construct a well-articulated answer. In the spirit, wait time allows believers to write the vision, consider the cost, and gain the fortitude necessary to produce excellence in the end results. Waiting works out the details, not just in what you produce, but in YOU.

#WorthTheWait

Decree: I do not mind waiting. I will be patient. I know my time is coming. When my time arrives, I will know it! I will not fear or become anxious as time moves. MY time belongs to me and I await it with expectation. I will flow in God's perfect timing for me.

THE **PUSH**

Pray	Plan	Reflect

_____

THE **PUSH**

Day 56 The Voice
John 1:22-23

In John 1:22-23, John declares who he is. In the face of many who wanted him to be something else, he is asked to give an account of himself. Who art thou? John calls himself a voice crying! Not a prophet, not the Christ, or another title or position. I wonder how many of us are willing to be a voice. Just a vessel used to say a word about God. Who is willing to cry for the people and speak life into them, even in the wilderness? John knew his assignment; he could articulate his role in the kingdom; and, he was not concerned with impressing people with a title but rather accomplishing his assignment. John's voice cried, it cared about the coming of the Lord, and preparing God's people for that day. John knew that his voice was a cry of preparation. He understood who he was and the role he was to play. He humbly submitted to achieving his purpose, knowing that Christ would come with a greater purpose (v.26-27). John stayed in his lane. Do you know your identity in Christ? What is your assignment in the kingdom? Could you be that voice God wants to use? Is there something God placed on the inside of you that needs to be spoken? Who will be more prepared because you cried?

#BeTheVoice

Decree: I will use my voice to prepare God's people. I will fulfill MY assignment. I know my role and I will stay in my lane!

THE **PUSH**

Pray	Plan	Reflect

_____
_____
_____
_____
_____
_____
_____
_____
_____
_____
_____
_____
_____
_____
_____
_____
_____
_____
_____
_____
_____
_____
_____
_____
_____
_____
_____

THE **PUSH**

Day 57 The Call
Exodus 3:11 & 4:1, Jeremiah 1:5-6 & Jonah 1:1-3

God calls the seemingly inadequate, unqualified, least likely, and the resistant. When God called Moses, Moses asked, "Who am I to go before the King?" Later he asked, "What will I say" (Exodus 3:11 & 4:1). When he called Jeremiah, Jeremiah stated, "I am young, so I cannot speak" (Jeremiah 1:5-6). When he called Jonah, Jonah went in a different direction (Jonah 1:1-3). Could He have called you? Not because you have it all together, but because He knows you will rely on Him and not yourself. You can run, but you can't hide. Say yes today. Knowing that if He calls you, He has already equipped you and requires you to depend on Him. Moses, Jeremiah, and Jonah went on to do great things. Their inadequacies did not prevent them from accomplishing what God assigned to them. I have met countless people who refuse to answer the call. What I have noticed is their unhappiness. People who are not walking in their God purpose are not happy. They have plenty of excuses, some blame, and some have a lot of concern for what others will do or think. God wants us to overcome these obstacles and walk in our God purpose. It's not too late! Answer the call! The truth is, you are not truly happy until you do.

#AnsweringTheCall

Decree: I will do what God has assigned to me! I believe God can use me with my inadequacies! Today, I say, yes Lord!

THE **PUSH**

Pray   **Plan**   **Reflect**

Day 58 Abundant Life
Deuteronomy 30:19

"I call heaven and earth to record this day against you, that I have set before you, life and death, blessing and curses: therefore, choose life, that both thou and thy seed may live".

Choosing life is an everyday, all day, each moment choice. Each day we are presented with opportunities to make choices that impact our future. Whether it is choosing between procrastination or pursuing our dreams or working out or laying on the couch. We all make choices. The choices we make effect our legacy, our children. We have the power to choose life.

Do not let another day go by with regrets or an, "I'll do it tomorrow" mindset. Choose today to have life--for Jesus came that we would have life abundantly. Living and existing are different. God desires that we choose life and LIVE. Live it to the fullest and in abundance. When we do so, we also bless our children with life.

#LiveLifeLoud

Decree: I will live! I choose life! I speak life! I no longer merely exist, I choose to live an abundant life! I free my children to live, by example!

THE **PUSH**

Pray   **Plan**   **Reflect**

_____

_____

_____

_____

_____

_____

_____

_____

_____

_____

_____

_____

_____

_____

_____

_____

_____

_____

_____

_____

_____

_____

_____

_____

_____

_____

_____

Day 59 Sacrifice of Praise
Isaiah 61:3 & Hebrews 13:15

Hebrews 13:15 declares, "By him therefore let us offer the sacrifice of praise to God continually, that is, the fruit of our lips giving thanks to His name". Have you told God you love him today? I know some of us may be going through a storm or experiencing some pain, but praise and worship can serve as warfare. If you learn to worship and praise God past your circumstances He will remove heaviness (Isaiah 61:3). The best praise is not given when everything is going right, it is when it looks bad, but you believe God enough to declare, He's able AND even if he doesn't do it in our time, He is still an awesome God. Feeling heavy and weighed down? Praise and worship Jesus Christ! God inhabits the praises of His people. He reveals himself during worship. We become closer to God through praise and worship. God provides clarity and peace in worship. Many of the answers we need can be heard during our worship. Many people pray every day and study consistently, but do not praise and worship God. These are not just external actions, but an internal attitude. It comes from a heart of adoration and gratefulness. In this season of your life, do not underestimate the need or power of praise and worship. Let God know you love Him, both in actions and character. You were created to worship. Do not wait another second, worship Him now. Open your mouth and heart to God.

#WinningInWorship

Decree: I was created to worship God. My worship draws God nearer. My praise and worship come from a heart of adoration and gratefulness.

THE **PUSH**

Pray	Plan	Reflect

Day 60 Cheerleaders
First Samuel 30:6

When many of us envision success, we picture celebrations with our friends, family and supporters around. We approach success much like basketball players prep for a game. We practice, often in private. We perform in front of crowds and we enjoy winning. However, there will come a time when you realize life is not a game. Unlike basketball or other sports, we will not have the support of cheerleaders on your side lines. In life we find that it doesn't always matter how many good friends you have. God often requires some level of isolation when He is preparing you for elevation. Even after your victory God will scatter and separate those you felt were needed. First Samuel 30:6 demonstrates that David understood this and thus encouraged himself in the Lord. At this point in the text, David's wife and children were taken captive, his home was burned down, and his own army was posturing to turn against him. (This was the future King David.) David's name was known in the kingdom, he was mighty in battle, yet he was isolated in a season when it would have been great to feel supported. The absence of fans does not mean you can forfeit what God has assigned to your hands. Today, be your biggest fan. Cheer yourself on. Tell yourself, I will make it. I will win. I am a conqueror, an overcomer, a victor, and my King has already won the battle. Iron your initials on your own shirt, grab some pom-poms and declare, "I'm on God's team and I cannot lose!"

#WinningTeam

Decree: I am on God's team and I cannot lose! I will encourage myself.

THE PUSH

Pray	Plan	Reflect

Day 61 God's Love
Romans 3:35-39

There is nothing that can separate us from the love of God. When we are in places of tribulation, we often think that it is an indication that God is angry or displeased with us. We equate receiving good things with being loved. God does not just love us through what He provides, but in how He prepares us. Tribulation does not separate us from God's love, it prepares us to be what He desires. Your present and past circumstances are not an indication of a separation from God. Nothing can separate you from His love. It is the enemy's job to attempt to convince you that you are unlovable. The enemy starts by reminding you of your shortcomings. This is followed by feelings of impatience and wondering why God has not done IT (insert your IT here we all have one) for you yet. He must be angry. You question how God can use or want someone like you. God loves us unconditionally and completely. He longs for us to accept that He loves us. Surrendering to God does not result in rejection, but rather connection. You are the apple of His eye. You are more than what you are facing, you are a conqueror and your Heavenly Father loves you so much. Nothing can separate you from God's love, not even you.

#NoGreaterLove

Decree: I am loved by God! His love for me is consistent! God loves me beyond my disappointments. Nothing can separate me from God's love.

THE **PUSH**

Pray   **Plan**   **Reflect**

Day 62 Our Infinite Source
John 10:10

When you begin to realize your worth, potential, and purpose in God, it will confirm that you are adequate in Him. What challenges this knowledge is focusing on what you are not as oppose to who is with you. You were never meant to know everything, have everything, and meet every need. Our inability to be all knowing can be frustrating. We want to have all the answers and solutions to our purpose and the path God has placed us on. When we do not we feel an urgency to be more and know more, we shift our efforts into intellectual preparation. We read books, attend classes, and seek help from advisors. While there is nothing wrong with the pursuit of knowledge, just know that you will never know everything. You do not know what the future holds. God has your future mapped out; every step of it. It is designed not only to prepare you mentally, but spiritually. Spiritual responses to life's dilemmas are transferrable, intellectual responses don't always have this perk. When you spend time in His presence (prayer, studying the word, etc.), God gives you discernment, strength, courage, and whatever else you need. So, it doesn't matter what life brings, you have the spiritual recipe to assist you with navigating your life. You will not be enough because of how intelligent you are, what you know, or who you know. You are enough because of your connection to an infinite, omnipotent, and omniscient God. He is the source for abundant living. If He is your source, you can live beyond adequacy and step into overflow. You have more than enough to get it done!

#InfiniteSource

Decree: I serve a God of overflowing provision. I am connected to an infinite source. My knowledge and abilities may be limited, but my God's are limitless. My God has given me more than enough power, strength, ability, and wisdom to do what He has called me to do. I am enough in Him!

THE PUSH

Pray   **Plan**   **Reflect**

Day 63 Restoration
Joel 2:25

If you are like me, you may feel that you have wasted years' operating as if you were not valuable. If you are not careful this can lead to regret and condemnation. Do not allow yourself to spend too much time worrying about the past. It is necessary to reflect to not repeating mistakes, but do not beat yourself up about it. In addition to God's grace, mercy, and favor, He is a restorer. God promises to restore the years that were eaten up along the way (Joel 2: 25). In addition, Psalms 23: 3 declares he can restore your very soul. Psalms 51:12 tells us that God will restore our joy, while Jeremiah 30: 7 reminds us that God is also a restorer of our health. Today believe that God is working on getting you back everything you lost or gave away. Don't worry about your past, press towards your future, God's already working for you!

#GodRestores

Decree: God is giving me back everything I need. He is restoring my time, my soul, my joy, my health, and everything else that was lost/taken from me. They belong to me. Today I take them back!

THE **PUSH**

Pray	Plan	Reflect

Day 64 Rejection
First John 3:1-2 & 16

In pursuit of your purpose you will experience rejection. You may not get the business loan, the owner of the building may deny you a lease, you may be told no again and again. You may even be rejected by friends. You may notice your inner circle leaving you out or not responding to your attempts at communication. If you are going to pursue what God has for you, rejection should be expected. The good news is, we serve a God who loves us and does not reject us. The Heavenly Father's love for us can seem a bit unnatural, because it is. It defies all the logical and worldly love we often experience. It may seem strange that God in His awesomeness, omnipotence, and omnipresence could love us. God does not just love us, He goes further to consider us sons and daughters. We may be rejected by people, but God is not like people. Our Lord and Savior understands rejection. He was rejected by the same people he came to save. Be encouraged! God loves you so much He gave up His son as a provision to your promise! You may be rejected by man, but accepted God.

#RejectionIsABlessing

Decree: I am accepted by God! Rejections will not hinder me! The world's no, is not a NO from God. God approves of me!

THE **PUSH**

Pray	Plan	Reflect

Day 65 Forward
Philippians 3:13-14 & Haggai 2:9

One major hindrance to forward progression is the past. We learn things both consciously and unconsciously. As we live, we adapt to things both good and bad. At times we become so accustomed to our past experiences, it is uncomfortable to walk in the newness of our future. I believe that is why Paul calls it a press. He understood that moving beyond the past is difficult. Don't look back! Everything God has for you is in front of you. Wasting time with, I could have, should have, or wish I would've.... will only slow down your momentum towards your promise. The past has taught you some truths, but it has also led to some false theories or lies about who you are and can be. Throw out the learning that does not align with the word of God for your life. Do not allow your experiences to trap you into a box of limitations, instead believe God despite what you have experienced. Trust Him and have faith; knowing that beyond this is a prize and a higher calling. Your future will be greater than your past!

#PressPassYourPast

Decree: I'm moving forward. I press beyond what has already occurred into the possibility in front of me. I will press through discomfort and beyond me.

THE PUSH

Pray   **Plan**   **Reflect**

Day 66 The Great Exchange
Isaiah 61:3 & Ezekiel 37:3

We are familiar with the world's system of exchange. Everything in our society operates based on equal exchange. When we return items to the store without a receipt, we are told to find something of equal or lesser value. When determining the value of an item, we ponder the cost. Is it worth what I will have to give up? God's exchange system is so revolutionary. He merely asks for what we have. Isaiah 61:3 declares that God gives beauty for ashes. This is amazing because ashes represent something that has been burned beyond recognition. It has been burned so much so that it is unrecognizable. It no longer looks like what it was. Many of us have been burned by life. We are left with the ashes of what use to be. For some, it's hard to let go of all they have left, even if what you have left is not working for them. Some of us cry in the ashes, others play in the ashes, but few of us give God the ashes. Giving God the ashes signify that you trust and believe in His power to do something miraculous with them. We do not have the power nor capacity to turn ashes into something beautiful. But God is asking you to give Him your burned, unrecognizable bodies, situations, past, failures, relationships, and watch Him make them beautiful. I ask you what God asked Ezekiel, "Can these dry bones live?"

#BeautyForAshes

Decree: Today I give God the ashes. I let go of what I don't have the power to fix. I believe and trust that God can make them beautiful. I let go!

THE PUSH

Pray   **Plan**   **Reflect**

_____

_____

_____

_____

_____

_____

_____

_____

_____

_____

_____

_____

_____

_____

_____

_____

_____

_____

_____

_____

_____

_____

_____

_____

_____

_____

_____

Day 67 Diamonds are Forever
Proverbs 31:10

The Bible tells us that the price or worth of a virtuous woman is far above rubies. Far above suggest a great distance between the women's worth and that of rubies. If you would allow me the creative liberty of examining the one stone that is valuable far above rubies; the diamond. Diamonds are found covered within the earth. They are created under pressure and heat. Diamonds are worth more than cubic zirconia because they are real- not man-made. They are a natural resource created by the Father's process. With close examination, it is not hard to see the connection between your own life and that of a diamond. The perfect balance of pressure, heat, and support, has created the gem that is you. The pressure was never meant to break you only to make you tougher, durable, and valuable. You are no cubic zirconia, you are the real deal! It took time to make you fabulous and strong. Though many have tried, all have failed to create the perfect process that produces you, only God can do that. Your value is beyond that of diamonds, guard it as such!

#Diamond

Decree: I am a diamond. I have worth and value. I will shine. I will guard myself as priceless.

THE **PUSH**

Pray	Plan	Reflect

Day 68 Forgiveness Part I
James 2:13

There is no room for partiality in the body of Christ. If we love God and wish to bring Him glory, we cannot withhold from some and freely distribute to others our love and forgiveness. John 2:13 reminds us that if we show mercy we shall receive mercy. That same chapter of scripture addresses treating all people the same, this includes those who have not treated us fairly. Leviticus 19:18 declares, "Thou shalt not avenge, nor bear any grudge against the children of thy people, but thou shalt love thy neighbor as thyself: I am the Lord". Loving your neighbor as you love yourself is mentioned several times in the bible. It is basic instruction to God's people. God has established our need to love others and treat them the way God treats us. In doing this, we meet His criteria to receive His love, forgiveness, and grace.

#EqualGrace

Decree: Lord, I will forgive! I will love everyone I encounter and examine my life for any area(s) of unforgiveness.

THE **PUSH**

Pray	Plan	Reflect

Day 69 Forgiveness Part II
Matthew 6:12-15

The level to which you can forgive is directly connected to the level of forgiveness you receive. In forgiving others, you not only release them, you release yourself. In freeing them from the penalty of their sin, you are freed from your own. One of the easiest ways to begin the forgiveness process is to attempt to identify how you may have hurt God in the same way the person or situation has hurt you. I have also found it helpful to consider the life of the one who has hurt me. Have they experienced hurt that has found a root, making it easy for them to hurt me. Hurt people really do hurt people. Are you requiring more of others than you are willing to give of yourself to God? Your release is waiting for you. Let it go!

#Release

Decree: Lord I release any hurt I have to you! I ask for forgiveness for my own sins and release those who have sinned against me from penalty.

THE **PUSH**

Pray	Plan	Reflect

Day 70 Forgiveness Part III
Luke 6:37-38

A measuring cup is used to determine the amount or how much of an ingredient that must be added to a recipe. In the same way, we must consider our measure of grace and forgiveness towards others. Do we distribute it generously and in return receive it generously? Do we do just enough to appear outwardly forgiving, yet our hearts remain cold towards individuals? We give just enough to be nice, but not enough to cover the grace we ourselves need. Consider your mistakes, failures, mishaps, and sins. How many cups would they fill? Use those same cups and fill them with love, grace, and forgiveness towards others. Pour it out with the same measure it was poured for you. Luke 12:48 declares, "… to whom much is given much is required…".

#EmptyCup

Decree: I can give and receiving love. I will give love. I will give grace. I will give mercy.

THE **PUSH**

Pray   **Plan**   **Reflect**

_____

_____

_____

_____

_____

_____

_____

_____

_____

_____

_____

_____

_____

_____

_____

_____

_____

_____

_____

_____

_____

_____

_____

_____

_____

_____

_____

_____

_____

_____

_____

_____

THE **PUSH**

Day 71 Forgiveness Part IV
Mark 11:24-26

God has not left you alone with the difficult task of forgiving. Meet Him in prayer so that His power can transform your heart, mind, and soul. You must seek God to forgive. Our flesh will resist forgiveness. It goes against our sin nature, but our spirit desires to be free. We must overcome our flesh with God's word. Our fleshly desires will not naturally subject themselves to our will to forgive. Forgiveness will not happen on its own. We must be intentional. We must dictate daily to our flesh, through the word of God that we will forgive. When hate, resentment, and forgiveness come up in our spirits, we must not give it a place (not even for a moment). Reject every thought that does not align with the mandate to forgive. Then replace it with a scripture or affirmation of your willingness and obedience to let it go! Confess God's word over your life. If God requires it, He has given you the power to do it! You are closer now than yesterday!

#REJECTreplace

Decree: I reject all bitterness, hate, and pain. I choose to forgive. I want to be more like Christ. I am obedient to His word. I let go! Through Christ I can do all things!

151

THE **PUSH**

Pray	Plan	Reflect

152

Day 72 Forgiveness Part V
Matthew 18:23-35

Think back to the weight and guilt you held before you committed your life to Jesus. For some, this may be long ago, yet for others, this may be today. When you accepted Jesus Christ as your Lord and Savior, you presented your sin sick soul and He forgave every sin you ever committed. He freed you from the guilt, shame, and penalty. You can now walk in liberty. Oh, what a gift, eternal life, unconditional love, and a clean slate! If you are like me, your sins were many and your debt great. Someone else needs to feel and experience that same change. Allow yourself to be the vehicle by which they are introduced to the forgiving power of Jesus. By releasing them, you may win their soul for Christ. You may not believe they should live guilt free. Remember, you didn't deserve your freedom, yet God's grace covered for you! Today is "show and tell" day. Show and demonstrate the forgiving power of God and go tell someone what He has done for you.

#Show&Tell

Decree: Today I will give someone the grace that was given to me! I will be merciful. I repent for holding others to debts that I myself didn't pay. I extend the same liberty given to me to them. I too did not deserve the amazing gift of grace given to me.

THE **PUSH**

Pray	Plan	Reflect

_____

_____

_____

_____

_____

_____

_____

_____

_____

_____

_____

_____

_____

_____

_____

_____

_____

_____

_____

_____

_____

_____

_____

_____

_____

_____

_____

154

Day 73 It's Bigger Than Me
Revelations 12:11

Often in life we face circumstances and trials with a self-centered perspective. We view life's challenges with questions like--Why me; which can lead to a 'victim' mindset. Instead, view obstacles as an opportunity to give God glory and become more equipped with the character needed to live in sustainable success in God. The bible says, in Romans 5:4, "...tribulation produces patience and patience produces hope". That hope will not embarrass or shame you. The challenge is not meant to break you but to make you stronger and wiser. When we emerge from the challenge with victory, we give other permission to do the same. Conquering what could have conquered us, births ministry and lessons that produce an authentic message. It also produces character that can keep you in the places that God is taking you. Prepare to tell someone how you made it over, up, and out, not in mere words but in action. Someone is waiting on you to make it and to overcome. Your testimony is needed in the kingdom. Could it be that your obstacles are giving birth to ministry? Could God be equipping you with the tools and skills necessary to show others the way out?

#BiggerThanME

Decree: I will get through this successfully. On the other side of this is a better me. I see myself stronger and wiser. My tribulation is producing patience and hope. I am creating a glorious testimony.

THE **PUSH**

Pray	Plan	Reflect

_____

_____

_____

_____

_____

_____

_____

_____

_____

_____

_____

_____

_____

_____

_____

_____

_____

_____

_____

_____

_____

_____

_____

_____

_____

_____

_____

_____

Day 74 I Look Forward to It
Philippians 3:13-14

The familiar expression "I look forward to it", almost serves as a prophetic message for our journey forward. The statement is personal as indicated by "I". It also signifies the importance of expectation using the word "look". To look is to gaze in a direction. To look is not to see. It is possible to gaze in a specific direction without ever seeing what you were looking for. The use of "it" allows us to plug in whatever IT is we aspire towards. In our walk with God, we must remain optimistic and keep strong faith even when it can't be seen. A faith that expects the Lord to show up at any moment. The apostle Paul provides guidance as we seek to move forward. We must forget the past and stretch towards the future. This means setting our sights on the future and not allowing what was meant to be left behind to make its way into our destiny. In this scripture the word press can mean to run swiftly. Paul instructs us to run towards our calling. Indeed, if God has called or invited us to a purpose we should RSVP, commit to attending, and LOOK FORWARD to IT!

#LookingForward

Decree: My past is behind me. I leave it there! I set my sights on what is before me and expect God to show up at any moment. I say yes to the calling of God and I won't turn back.

THE **PUSH**

Pray	Plan	Reflect

THE **PUSH**

Day 75 Direction & Focus
Psalms 121:1-2

Moving forward is not without barriers and obstacles. In fact, these attempts to stifle and block our advancement should be expected. These challenges produce strength that will be necessary to sustain us as we achieve our goals. It is ironic that David speaks of lifting his eyes to see a hill. For many a hill would represent an obstacle or barrier to forward progression. However, here David acknowledged that the hill is where his help comes from. Instead of running from the challenge, look it head on, and don't turn back. Just believe that where there is a hill, the Lord is there. You were made to climb the hills of life. You were made to see its potential effects and apply your faith in the Lord. The same God that made the hill is God enough to take you over it or move it! When you really understand this concept, you will ask to be challenged because you know it produces growth. Like Joshua 14:12-15 you can declare, "Give me this mountain!"

#GiveMeMyMountain

Decree: Lord give me every opportunity to grow into the person I need to be to please you. Give me my mountain, my hill, and the challenges that are assigned to produce good and prune the bad. I will look to the hills and see my help.

THE **PUSH**

Pray	Plan	Reflect

_____

_____

_____

_____

_____

_____

_____

_____

_____

_____

_____

_____

_____

_____

_____

_____

_____

_____

_____

_____

_____

_____

_____

_____

_____

_____

_____

_____

THE **PUSH**

Day 76 It's Not a Problem, It's a Promotion
First Samuel 17:48-50

When David arrived at the scene of this war, he was bothered by the complacency of his people. The Philistine's big man had been taunting them for days. This produced fear in the children of Israel. The magnitude of the brother left them stuck and unwilling to defeat a battle whose victory belonged to them. Don't leave your battle unfought and your victory unfinished. His brothers appeared afraid of the Philistine Goliath, but David viewed him as beatable. He believed he possessed what was needed to defeat this giant. And defeat Goliath he did!!! David's courage in the face of fear established him as both a warrior and a leader. This victory served as the experience David needed to establish his resume to be king. Goliath was not a problem, he was a promotion. Could it be that what you view as a giant in your life, is an opportunity for you to develop the skills necessary to make it to the next level? It is all in your perspective. View obstacles as opportunities to develop, become strong, and establish a dependence on God. It's not a problem, it's a possibility for a promotion.

#Promotion

Decree: This seemingly big obstacle is my training ground. I serve a God who has defeated big obstacles. I serve a death defeating God. I have changed my mind. This battle is not a problem, it's a promotion.

THE **PUSH**

Pray	Plan	Reflect

Day 77 No Longer Empty
Ruth 1:20-22

The familiar book of Ruth is often told with much of the focus given to the relationship between Ruth and Boaz. However, there is a significant relationship between Ruth and Naomi. In the first chapter of Ruth, Naomi experiences a great loss. She loses her husband followed by the death of her two sons. In addition, to this grief, Naomi was left with two daughters-in-law and the land was experiencing a famine. The amount of grief, weight of responsibility, and the feeling of loss must have been no less than tumultuous. Given the situation Naomi decides to return home but expresses a bit of embarrassment. Naomi declares in Ruth 1:21 as she returns to her homeland that she went out full but returns empty. Have you ever left a place of comfort and provision and transitioned into a place of lack? I am sure she left home with dreams and a bright hope for your life. We all have experienced times when what we depended on can no longer sustain us.

The chapter goes on to say that Ruth and Naomi arrive at her home during the time of the barley harvest (Ruth 1: 22). What appeared to be a curse was a set up for increase. You cannot beat God's timing. Naomi and Ruth arrive right on time. They do not arrive in the middle of the harvest, nor at the end, but at the beginning. This means that God orchestrated the timing so that they could reap all that was available. Even in loss, grieving, and in times of famine, God loves us and cares about us. He is not done! Instead of drowning in sorrow and soaking in your grief, cry and move on. There is glory in the land God has for you. Many of us stay in the land of famine blaming God for the lack. Instead, let's trust God. The location you are in now might be experiencing a famine, but where God is taking you, you are just in time for the harvest. Ruth left where she was empty and returned in time for God to refill her again. Declare, "I've left my place of empty!"

THE **PUSH**

#NoLongerEmpty

Decree: I am no longer empty. I left that place for the harvest God has prepared for me. I will no longer drown in empty promises, empty conversation, or be afraid of empty threats. God has provided fullness for me; fullness of joy, fullness of peace, and fullness of provision.

THE **PUSH**

Pray	Plan	Reflect

THE **PUSH**

Day 78 Faith

Genesis 15:1, Numbers 21:34, Isaiah 7:4, Psalms 27:3, Luke 1:13 & 30 & Acts 27:24

When God plants vision that exceeds the believer's expectations, He tells them two words, "Fear not"! These words have been told to Abram (Gen 15:1), Moses (Numbers 21:34), Isaiah (Isaiah 7:4), David (Psalms 27:3), Zacharias (Luke 1:13), Mary (Luke 1:30), and Paul (Acts 27:24); just to name a few. It is evident that God knew and found it necessary to give this advice after equipping these change-making visionaries with an assignment. God knew the promise, vision, and destiny was gigantic. But, if you look back over your life, the smaller mountains were preparation. David killed a lion before Goliath, he protected sheep before becoming a king who protected God's people. The feeling of fear does not have to paralyze us, it can propel us! Don't stop your pursuit of God because you are afraid. I say to you what God said to them, "Fear not!" He told David not to fear the opposition. He told Zacharias, husband of barren Elisabeth, not to fear the appearance of the angel of the Lord in the middle of his barren and untimely situation. He told Mary to fear not when she became troubled after the angel addressed her a highly favored and blessed among women, when she had yet to bare a seed. He told Paul to fear not while amid a ship wreck. He told (insert name here) to fear not .... And you too will make it out with a glorious testimony! If he showed it to you, Go Get It! Fear not!

#FearNOT!

Decree: I will not be afraid. I will go forward without fear of opposition, lack, time, and circumstance.

166

THE **PUSH**

Pray	**Plan**	**Reflect**

Day 79 Healing
Psalms 147:3

Where do broken hearts go? The world has introduced many ways to manage pain. Most of us are not satisfied with managing pain, we want and need total healing. The world offers drugs, alcohol, and various medications, while these are temporarily effective at masking symptoms, they do not result in complete healing. Self- medication leads to addictions causing hope for wholeness to flee. In some cases, healing from physical wounds is easier than healing a broken heart. A broken heart can result in physical, emotional, and spiritual pain. Pain can cause you to lack focus and enthusiasm for life. Many people want to rush the process and quickly move on with life, carrying the pain from the past into the future. But there is good news!

Psalms 147:3 says, "He healeth the broken in heart, and bindeth up their wounds. God heals us and covers our wounds". By covering them, He prevents infection, further pain, and spreading of gems. Do not be left uncovered, letting the hurt seep out onto everyone you encounter. Do not allow the pain to get worse with time, instead of better. Do not self-medicate when God is the real pain killer, deliverer, and healer! He not only heals you, but He fills the void and puts it all back together again. Pray in faith for healing! Pray, God heal my broken heart and bind up my wounds. You can be healed.

#Don'tManageWhatYouCanBeDeliveredFrom

Decree: My heart is being healed and my wounds are covered. I will not walk into my next with the hurt of the past. I will not allow my hurt to make me hurt others. I am healed.

THE **PUSH**

Pray   **Plan**   **Reflect**

Day 80 Glory to God
Proverbs 16:18-19

Give glory to God! In life we all accomplish things and pursue greatness; however, your achievements are never really yours. Glory belongs to God! Proverbs 16:18 says, "Pride goeth before destruction, and a haughty spirit before a fall". When we get "the big head", we feel that we have arrived or believe we can do it without God. This is a sure path to destruction and a fall. Proverbs goes on to say that it is better to be humble! When you understand that the grace of God allows you to look good, you cannot get prideful, you must become more grateful! 2 Corinthians 12:9 states, "...my grace is sufficient for thee: for my strength is made perfect in weakness...". God has graced us with the ability to achieve and pursue dreams and passions that are beyond our reach, greater than our educational levels, and at times out of the scope of our vision. His grace is and always will be sufficient. We must remember that without God we are not able to be everything we can be. God is opening doors and taking us to great heights in Him. We must remain humble to maintain and sustain our place in the kingdom.

#StayHumble

Decree: Lord, keep me mindful of your grace. I thank you for the grace to do all that you have assigned to me. Help me to remain humble.

THE **PUSH**

Pray	Plan	Reflect

Day 81 Another Way
John 5:1-9

John 5:1-9 tells of a man at the pool of Bethesda. The man had an infirmity and was impotent (helpless and powerless) for 38 years. He was waiting at the pool for the angel to trouble the waters. Only the first to get into the pool to receive their healing. But, Jesus became another way! So often we limit ourselves to one way of being healed, blessed, and delivered. We assume that if God delivered someone that way, He will deliver us that way too. We think God is limited to operating within the scope of our knowledge. God is not restricted in His ability to heal us. He can do what He wants, however He wants. We create limitations, not God. Could it be that we have been waiting for years beside something we thought had to be taken care of in the only way we knew? Take a moment to reflect on the limitations we may have set. The man at the pool waited for 38 years for something he could have received in another way. He did not have to waste his time doing it the way everyone else did. Jesus was another way! He is waiting to be another way for us. Our creator is the master of another way. Instead of requiring God to do it our way, why not just let Him do it! We could sit and wait for 38 years for the only way WE know, while God has prepared another way for us.

#TakeTheLimitsOff

Decree: God I am open to receiving healing, deliverance, provision and whatever you have for me in unique ways. I expect opportunities from unusual and unlikely sources. I will not remain stuck in one way of thinking. I will not box God into my limited knowledge. Have Your way God! You are limitless!

THE **PUSH**

Pray   **Plan**   **Reflect**

Day 82 Teachable
Hebrews 12:5-11

I correct my children because I care about them. I am concerned with how certain behaviors will impact their future. Correcting them is not being mean; it is a sign of caring. So, it is with God! Hebrews 12:5-11 reminds us that He chastens those He loves. He disciplines and instructs us to bring us to an expected end. He knows what we need to be to do better. His correction is not to condemn, but to convict and correct. If God is correcting us, it is because He cares. It is necessary for us to have certain characteristics and skills for where God is taking us. He knows exactly what we need for where we are going. We must remain teachable, so we can learn and gain wisdom. Adhere to His guidance in your life, even when it hurts. If you did not pass the obedience test the first time, there will be a makeup test. He cares too much to let us ruin our future. He is the ultimate Father, Provider, Protector, and Promoter.

#Teachable

Decree: I am teachable! I can receive and adhering to correction. I will not become rebellious or feel defeated because of my mistakes. I am committed to making the changes needed for a better tomorrow. I know my Heavenly Father corrects me because He loves me!

THE **PUSH**

Pray	Plan	Reflect

Day 83 Beauty
Psalms 139:14

Lupita Nyong'o was named People's Most Beautiful Person in 2014. When receiving her Oscar, she revealed that she grew up being teased for the color of her skin. In interviews, she talked about not feeling pretty in her past. Psalms 139:14 states that we are fearfully and wonderfully made. It also declares that God's work on us is marvelous. Do not let the opinions of others determine how you view yourself. People are fickle, and everyone has an opinion. Seasons change and what is reverenced one day is mocked the next. What matters most is what you see when you look in the mirror. It matters what God says about you. They may not see your beauty, but during the day you cannot see the stars, it does not mean they aren't there. See the beauty in yourself. Do not examine yourself for every imperfection or compare yourself to others. You were created to be you and God said it was good.

#Beautiful

Decree: I am fearfully and wonderfully made. I was created purposefully the way that I am. I love myself. I am beautiful!

THE **PUSH**

Pray   **Plan**   **Reflect**

_____
_____
_____
_____
_____
_____
_____
_____
_____
_____
_____
_____
_____
_____
_____
_____
_____
_____
_____
_____
_____
_____
_____
_____
_____
_____
_____
_____
_____

THE **PUSH**

Day 84 When the Enemy Comes
Second Chronicles 32:1-8

In Second Chronicles 31:1-8 Hezekiah, King of Judah, learns that his enemy is coming. What do you do when you know your enemy is coming? Do you have enough discernment to know before he is walking in your back door? Hezekiah knew and did three powerful things. 1) He cut off the enemy's supply of water. He wasn't going to let the enemy be nourished by what belonged to his people. We must stop feeding the enemy with our negative words, doubts, and sin! Do not give him room. Do not water what you do not want to grow. Fill yourself with positivity and the word of God. 2) Hezekiah strengthened the walls! When you know you have an enemy, you cannot have breaches in your walls. You must keep yourself protected. Strengthen your walls with prayer, fasting, and praise. 3) He made an abundance of darts and shields. Do not just sit there! Prepare your weapon for the fight! Sharpen your sword. Get ready!

#Prepare

Decree. I am prepared for my enemy. My walls are built, and my weapon is sharp!

THE **PUSH**

Pray   **Plan**   **Reflect**

Day 85 Mistakes and Correction
Second Samuel 12:1-20

Second Samuel 12:1-7 tells of a major mistake David made in his life. Even though God blessed David with so much. He still desired things outside of God's will. Don't we all? In David's pursuit he sinned! God required a wage of death for that sin. David; 1) admitted he was wrong and repented, 2) fasted, 3) took his consequences, and, 4) got up and worshipped. Too many of us get slack when God corrects us, disciplines us, and points out our sin. Deal with sin or sin will deal with you. Sin does have a cost, but God's love offers us repentance and forgiveness. Don't leave church, get stuck in your mess, or fail to move on in ministry because you made a mistake. Repent and get up! Continue to worship God and be grateful for His care and correction. The Lord requires more of you and has not changed His mind about your destiny.

#Don'tSitInSin

Decree: I repent for anything I did that is displeasing to God. I repent for anything I should have done that I omitted to do. I am committed to doing better. Thank you, Lord, for your grace and mercy.

THE **PUSH**

Pray   **Plan**   **Reflect**

Day 86 Debt Relief
Nehemiah 1:11

Nehemiah was a cupbearer. This position of service to the king was a high honor. Nehemiah was charged with tasting wine before the king to ensure he would not be poisoned. Thanks be to God that Jesus became our cupbearer (Matthew 26)! He took the weight, shame, and guilt so that we might live free! Why then are we bound? He took the cup! He stands between us and the enemy. The price has been paid in full! He paid what we could not to give us what we do not deserve. Don't drink from the cup of mediocrity. That cup does not belong to you.

#TheCupThatPassed

Decree: Thank you God for bearing my cup. Thank you for paying the debt I owed. I will live to show you both appreciation and gratitude.

THE PUSH

Pray   **Plan**   **Reflect**

_____

_____

_____

_____

_____

_____

_____

_____

_____

_____

_____

_____

_____

_____

_____

_____

_____

_____

_____

_____

_____

_____

_____

_____

_____

_____

_____

_____

Day 87 Higher Calling
Matthew 19:23-26

Matthew 19:23-26 indicates it is difficult for a rich man to enter heaven, but not impossible. With so much prosperity preaching, we must be careful that we live balanced lives. It should never be about money, power, or fame in ministry! To prevent that, our prayers should not end at God provide opportunities and assignments, but God allow us to have integrity, character, and be a representative of His heart on Earth. No, we will not be perfect, but there is no need to rush into what appears to be a blessing and end up a curse because of our lack of integrity or compassion. It is difficult for a rich man to get into heaven because he/she must be willing to give it all up upon request. Attachment to the things of this world can be a hindrance in ministry. Whatever God gives, we must be willing to sacrifice for the sake of the cross and God's glory. It is essential that we not become so attached to the blessing and a certain level of lifestyle that we make decisions solely to sustain them. Ministry requires selflessness and sacrifice. God's provision should not distract you from the ultimate cause of Christ--to see the lost found and the blind able to see.

#BeyondProvision

Decree: I will not become so in love with your gifts that I neglect to stay in love with the gift giver. I will seek the kingdom. I am a person of integrity.

THE **PUSH**

Pray **Plan** **Reflect**

Day 88 Recycling God's Way
Jeremiah 18:4

God recycles! Jeremiah 18:4 gives the example of the potter who noticed an imperfection, left the clay in his hand, and used the same clay to make the vessel again, as He pleased. Isn't it good to know you are still in His hands? Just like the clay, we have imperfections, but when we remain in God's hands there is always opportunities to be made over. The Potter did not get new clay, He simply used what He already had. Let God make you again, as it pleases him. Imagine how the clay must feel, probably uncomfortable, but still in His hands. It is good to know that when we make mistakes, God can recycle what is flawed. He can recycle our marriages, our finances, and our lives, using us for His purpose. What God has inside of you can still be used.

#SameSubstanceDifferentProduct

Decree: Make me over God. If there is anything in me that does not belong, make me over. I submit to you pushing out the foreign substances and pouring in whatever makes me pliable. Keep me in Your hands.

THE **PUSH**

Pray	Plan	Reflect

Day 89 Here Comes The Rain!
Acts 14:17

Here comes the rain! Biblically, among other things, rain relates to fruit, increase, and seed. James 5:18 states that rain caused the earth to bear fruit. Acts 14:17 declares that after the rain there shall be a fruitful season. Isaiah 55:10 notes that rain causes the Earth to bring forth and sprout, giving seed to the sower. Lev. 26:4 further declares that rain causes the land to yield increase and fruit. That's good news! So, it is with us. In seasons of rain and storms, we are really being prepared to bear fruit, increase, sprout, and get seed to sow. The same rain that ruins our plans and causes floods, is also necessary for our growth and development. Without rain there we miss out on fruits, vegetables, and rich soil. Without rain our souls become dry places. Instead of hating the rain and storms in our lives, we should view them as seasons necessary for healthy production. Get excited about the rain. When you hear rain, you hear growth. I see God raining in your life.

#AfterTheRain

Decree: The storm and the rain were designed for my growth. I hear rain coming. I see me growing and producing what God has given me. The rain shall not stop me but sustain me! Here comes the rain.

THE **PUSH**

Pray	Plan	Reflect

THE **PUSH**

Day 90 Pray
Matthew 14:23 & 26:36-39

Living in this fast-paced society, where being busy is often viewed as a sign of success. It is essential that believers take time to pull away from it all and PRAY. It is key when to find moments of alone time with God when seeking God for answers to life's questions, needing direction, making decisions, etc. Get away from the noise of people's opinions and influence. Jesus himself understood this. In Matthew 14:23 & 26:36-39, He got away from the crowd and prayed. Be alone, be still, and pray. Then, be quiet. Do not move on without hearing what the Lord has to say. Do not seek the opinion or counsel of others before you seek God's. Stand guard against things that can alter your perspective and perception, such as ungodly counsel. God will reveal counselors, prayer partners, and those to connect with. Do not rob yourself of the push, progress, preparation, passion, and peace found in prayer.

#Pray

Decree: I am encircled by a great, powerful, Godly circle of influence. I am disciplined enough to set aside alone time to pray. My prayers are powerful and life changing, not just for me, but for others. I am a mighty prayer warrior with the ability to alter the course of life through my prayers.

THE **PUSH**

Pray	Plan	Reflect

Day 91 Praise Attracts
Psalms 33:1

Psalms 33:1 declares that we should, "Rejoice in the Lord, O ye righteous: for praise is COMELY for the upright". Comely means attractive, which means having beneficial qualities or features that induce someone to accept what is being offered. You could say praise is irresistible attraction. Praise is not limited to dance and mere words. Praise and worship is a lifestyle. Praise will attract. When Christ is lifted, He draws. Our praise, love, and compassion should draw people to us if we are Christians (Christ-like). Our praise and worship will draw our blessings to us. If your disposition says you do not like people and hate life, that is not the countenance of a believer. It will also serve as a barrier to receiving all the good that is awaiting you. Let's make our walk COMELY!

#WorkingOnMyWitness

Decree: My praise attracts people to the God in me. My praise drowns out negativity and sadness. My praise draws good things to my life. I will praise the Lord for He is great!

THE PUSH

Pray   **Plan**   **Reflect**

Day 92 Goals
Philippians 3:12-14 & Habakkuk 2:2

What are your goals? Have you written them down? Have you considered the objectives that must be met for your goals to be reached? Today, consider Philippians 3:12-14 and "press towards a goal". Follow the guidance of Habakkuk 2:2 and "write the vision". Put your goals, objectives, and vision on paper. Consider adding a timeline for each objective and a date for each overall goal. Make plans to take a step each day towards your goal. Some steps may be small, while others may be larger. That's okay. It does not matter the size of the step, if it takes you forward, it is progress. The key is to place action behind every step of your goal. Little by little, you will begin to accomplish your goal if you take small steps in a predetermined direction. Do something towards your vision every day. Fill out the application, start editing your resume, go on a walk, write one page of the book, do something! Trust God that the vision will be completed (Philippians 1:6). While considering your goals and vision remember that we are charged with helping others. Be sure to include how you will give back to your community and reach out to others to help achieve the same success you have accomplished.

#GoalsToReach

Decree: I will take one step towards accomplishing my goals today. I am committed to doing something every day that takes me closer to my destination. I am disciplined and committed.

THE **PUSH**

Pray	Plan	Reflect

Day 93 Sowing & Reaping
Galatians 6:7 & Second Corinthians 9:10

Galatians 6:7 tells us that whatever we sow, we reap. This is true of both negative and positive things. Whatever we put out is what we get back. If we are inconsistent in our sowing, our reaping will be inconsistent. This is not just true for money, but also love, kindness, and the fruits of the spirit. It is important that we sow what we wish to reap. No one sows watermelon seeds expecting pumpkins! We must not sow time and expect money. Do not sow gossip and expect everyone to stay out of your business. Do not sow seeds of lies and then wonder why people lie on you. Sow joy, money, love, friendship, and loyalty and you will get them back. Do it consistently and they will come back consistently. A consistent seed produces consistent harvest. What you have now is a result of what you sowed yesterday. The blessing is that God will multiply your seed sown. God will multiply your resources. He does not judge the seed, He increases your harvest.

#SowSoItWillGrow

Decree: Today, I start consistently sowing great things. I plant seeds of love, joy, and faithfulness. I am in a position to harvest great things.

Pray   **Plan**   **Reflect**

_____

_____

_____

_____

_____

_____

_____

_____

_____

_____

_____

_____

_____

_____

_____

_____

_____

_____

_____

_____

_____

_____

_____

_____

_____

_____

_____

_____

_____

_____

_____

_____

Day 94 Strength
Isaiah 40:29

Isaiah 40:29 says, "He giveth power to the faint; and to them that have no might he giveth strength". Are you feeling faint (weak, dizzy, and close to losing consciousness)? There's good news! He gives power (the ability and capacity to do) to the faint. Do you lack might (force, energy, or an impressive power)? There is more good news! He gives strength to the weak. In fact, it is in our weakness that His power is made perfect (2 Corinthians 12:9-11)! Give Him your weakness and he will provide strength, win the battle, and give you the victory. Feeling a lack of strength is not an indication that you need to stop. It could mean you need to rest. Avoid making key decisions when you are feeling weak. Instead, get the rest you need, spend some time in prayer, and get back to it! When you have come to the end of you, God is just getting started!

#StrengthIsComing

Decree: Weakness is temporary. I can be rejuvenated, refreshed, and revived in God's presence. I will rest and press on!

THE **PUSH**

Pray　　　　　　　**Plan**　　　　　　　**Reflect**

THE **PUSH**

Day 95 God's Choice
First Samuel 16:1-13

First Samuel 16:1-13 tells of Samuel's visit to Jesse's house to anoint the next king. In verse seven, Samuel believes that one son looks like he should be anointed king, but God says no. God looks at the heart not the outward appearance. If that is what God does, shouldn't we do the same? We must be careful not to determine someone's anointing by our standards. Anointing does not have to be pretty, but it does have to come with POWER! Don't block your blessing judging people by how they appear outwardly. God may send someone that does not meet your standards but has His power. David was not the first choice of man, not even the second choice, but He was God's choice. Maybe you feel looked over or left out. Remember, David's own father did not originally mention him. When others fail to see the king or queen in you, God can send confirmation and approval despite them. Samuel was not willing to even sit until he discovered the king God had appointed. God uses the least likely, the overlooked, and the pushed aside. God's anointing rests on whoever He selects, and He does not need our approval to do it!

#AnointedByGod

Decree: I am a discerner of God's anointing. I look deeper than the surface of man. I am anointed and chosen by God. I walk in the oil of the anointing that rests on me now and forever.

THE **PUSH**

Pray   **Plan**   **Reflect**

Day 96 Double for Your Trouble
Isaiah 61:7

Have you ever experienced public humiliation? Have you felt ashamed of your current situation? Have you experienced peoples' harsh criticism and attempts to diminish and ruin your character? Well I have good news, Isaiah 61:7 says you will receive double for your shame! Double the anointing, double the opportunities, double blessing, double the elevation, and double doors!!! Double!!! I know you have cried, tossed and turned, feared your fate, and wondered why. Do not let the shame stop you. Do not count yourself out. Your dilemma has set you up for double. His plan has you winning. Double your expectations and get ready!

#DoubleForYourTrouble

Decree: I will not walk in shame. My shame has positioned me for double. God has not changed His mind concerning His promises. I walk in favor.

THE **PUSH**

Pray   **Plan**   **Reflect**

Day 97 God's Will
Matthew 6:10

We often pray for things that are not aligned with God's will for our lives. The results can lead us down the wrong road and cause detours in our lives. We will still get to the place God has promised, but it may take longer. When you have experienced praying for something, getting it, only to find out that it makes you miserable, feels like a weight, and appears to cause more damage than good, you learn to pray, "thy will be done" (Matthew 6:10). God's will, will never be wrong, tainted by pride, ego, or people pleasing. His will is always right. You cannot go wrong asking for God's will. God's will be often in opposition with our flesh. Our flesh wants the easy way, the people pleasing way, or the way that makes us appear to have advanced. God's will often require faith, does not please people, and is aimed at advancing you internally and externally.

#HisWill

Decree: Lord, at times I think I know what I want and need. Today I ask for your will for my life to be done. Have your way in my life. I give you complete control of my destiny.

THE **PUSH**

Pray	Plan	Reflect

THE **PUSH**
Day 98 Triumph Over Trials
First Peter 4:12-13

Everyone has a process, a journey, a cross, and trials. When we are in the thick of our own issues and dilemmas, it often feels like everyone else is doing great. It is not that everyone else has it all together. It is just that some have learned how to live under pressure through faith. Do I experience fear? Yes! Have I lost a lot? Been hurt before? Felt like giving up? Yes, yes, and yes. But what I hold onto is that my trials have the power to break me or make me! I Peter 4:12-13 tells us that trials are not strange. How you view them will determine how you come out of them. I believe every test and trial is a lesson to equip me to be better and do better. Do not let what was meant to build you be an excuse to self-destruct. You will make it!

#Endurance101

Decree: I am better because of my trials! I am learning, growing, and becoming wise through this! I will make it!

THE **PUSH**

Pray	Plan	Reflect

_____
_____
_____
_____
_____
_____
_____
_____
_____
_____
_____
_____
_____
_____
_____
_____
_____
_____
_____
_____
_____
_____
_____
_____
_____
_____
_____
_____

THE **PUSH**

Day 99 Work in Progress
Ephesians 2:10

Ephesians 2:10 declares that we are the Lord's workmanship, created for good works that we should walk in. The great thing about workmanship is that God has His creation in a process. He is skilled enough to complete it and we should walk in what He creates for us. We should guard against coveting the gifts and workmanship of others. We can admire what God has given others, but we should not be jealous or envious over what God has given to someone else. In doing so, we indicate that what He has given to us is not enough. Instead, we must inspect the valuable workmanship He has created in us and honor Him for putting wonderful treasures in earthen vessels.

Being His workmanship and created for good works also means we must trust in God's process. We must believe that each step, every trial, and even complicated situations are opportunities to do good works. Walk it out! We should be uncomfortable walking after bad works. We were not created for that! You are created to accomplish great things! Knowing this, we must allow His hands to mold us – His word to convict us – and His love to engulf us. Let's walk in our God-created good works and let our light shine!

#Workmanship

Decree: I am being worked on by God! I have been created to accomplish good works! I will walk in what I was created to be! I only desire to be HIS workmanship, not that of another. I desire to be me.

208

THE **PUSH**

Pray   **Plan**   **Reflect**

THE **PUSH**

Day 100 Kingdom Within Us
Luke 17:20-21

Luke 17:20-21 informs us that the Kingdom of God is not in a place and cannot be seen by observation. This scripture tells us that the Kingdom of God is within us. God's agenda, assignment, and purpose are inside of us. We must seek to fulfill this assignment for His kingdom to come and His will to be done. We are ambassadors who serve to fulfill God's wishes on earth. This means that what God wants to fulfill in His kingdom is planted in us. Each believer holds a piece of the puzzle to build the complete plan. Do not let a piece be missing because you just cannot believe that He has chosen you to fulfill His agenda on earth. The fact that He has placed these treasures in earthly vessels is incredible and humbling. Do not just sit with an assignment that will benefit God's people and do nothing! His grace is sufficient to help us carry out the assignment. His kingdom is in us.

#KingdomAssignment

Decree: I am important to the plan of God! My assignment is needed in the kingdom.

THE **PUSH**

Pray	Plan	Reflect

Day 101 Stay Focused
Hebrews 12:1

Distractions are defined as things that prevents someone from giving their full attention to a specific thing. We can be distracted by people, places, and things. Distractions don't scream, "Hey be distracted by me. I'll slow your progress down!" No! Sometimes distractions are unchecked seeds that have been planted in your mind, in your past, small time wasters, and even so called fun. The bible tells us that weight and sin can be distractions (Hebrews 12:1). In the text, it says these things easily beset us. Beset means to threaten persistence. In other words, don't let your desire for forbidden things threaten your persistence. Sin often has a pull to it. It pulls you away from God through the lust of your flesh. It is impossible to pursue God and sin at the same time. In this way, sin and weight are distractions to our progress. They can cripple our ability to persist. If you have a God-given goal, let nothing and no one beset you!

#ClearFocus

Decree: I am persistent, focused, and resilient! I lay aside every weight and sin in my life! I am in pursuit of something bigger than me! I am focused and undistracted.

THE **PUSH**

Pray   Plan   Reflect

213

Day 102 Seasons
Ecclesiastes 3:1

Ecclesiastes 3:1 teaches us that "To everything there is a season, A time to every purpose under the sun". Our lives have seasons and between each season, we experience transitions and change. We each have purpose. Our purpose requires God's timing. If you are in a season of discomfort and chaos, don't be alarmed. Seasons change! If you are concerned about the "whens" in life, like when should I start it, when is it going to change, and when is it going to get better, know that your problems have an expiration date and your purpose is set. Soon the greenest leaves change colors and fall to the ground and the cycle begins again.

The key here is to recognize what season you are in and plan accordingly while prepping for your next season. When we know winter is coming we get ready. We may buy a coat, check our tires, test our heating system, etc. This is done because we already know what types of conditions may occur during the winter season. We don't wait to prepare once the first big snow storm hits. We manage the shift through proper preparation. When the season ends, we do not throw away the coat. Just as in the physical, so it is in the spiritual. When our seasons end, we should not throw away what we have learned. This would be insane. Instead, we store it because we know that season could come around again. The more we learned in the last cycle/season, the less taxing we will find the new season.

Do a careful inspection of the spiritual season you are in, make adjustments, and live in it victoriously. Are you in a season of letting go or attaining? Is this your season to cry or your season to leap with joy? Embrace the season you are in and live! Can you imagine how you would react to someone wearing a swimsuit in a snow storm? This is an illustration of how we look when we do not live according to our season. Focus on what God is doing in your life during times of just enough and/or times of plenty. Get the lesson and LIVE victorious! In other words, don't spend when it's your season to save or save when it's time to invest.

You may be experiencing a season of financial plenty. It does not mean you should increase your spending. It means prepare for seasons when resources may be few. You may even be in a time of lack. During these seasons, do not just sit there crying about your current circumstance. Use this season to develop a plan and prepare your priorities knowing that this too shall pass. Get ready for a shift in your seasons!

God will ring the alarm and you will, in the right time, walk into your next season. There is so much wisdom and value in identifying your season and living accordingly. Seasons change. Your time is coming!

#Transitions

Decree: I know what season I'm in! I know how to live according to the season. I am prepared for my next season.

THE **PUSH**

Pray	Plan	Reflect

Day 103 Restoration
Job 42:10 & Joel 2:23-26

Job 42:10 says, "And the Lord turned the captivity of Job, when he prayed for his friends; also the Lord gave Job twice as much as he had before.
I know we all have our own issues to pray for, but I implore you to go before God for someone else. Job was restored and delivered after praying for his friends. With all the loss that Job experienced, most would understand why he did get selfish in his prayer life. We are often so focused on our own issues, we do not consider that we may be better off than others. Even with the circumstances of his own life, Job decided to pray for someone else. In doing so, Job was rewarded with restoration. Could it be that our lack of recovery is due to our own inability to consider others and be grateful and content in ALL things? I am reminded that even as Jesus hung on the cross, He chose to pray for those who placed him there.

Joel 2: 23-26 reminds us that God is in the restoration business. God can send you the stored-up blessings and the current blessings all at once. This text tells us to rejoice! God can restore anything you have lost. I know you feel you have wasted time, energy, and effort, but don't worry He can restore years. Whatever you lost God has an incredible insurance plan and will replace, restore, and replenish it all. Rejoice! Keep holding on, He is restoring what was taken away, what was given away, and what you didn't even know you were missing! He is the God that gave Job double!

#HeIsRestoring #PrayersThatRestore

Decree: I will pray for others. I am grateful. I can and will be restored! I expect DOUBLE!

THE **PUSH**

Pray   Plan   Reflect

Day 104 Out of the Darkness
Matthew 10:27

Matthew 10:27, "What I tell you in darkness that speak ye in light: and what ye hear in the ear, that preach ye upon the housetops".

God speaks in our darkest hours. We must not let His voice be drowned out by our own fears and depression. It is in our darkest times that God gives us wisdom. We must listen. What He tells us in these times is meant to be shared with others so that they too can make it out. I thank God He speaks in the dark times--leading and guiding when we cannot see our way. Follow His voice. Preachers and teachers, preach and teach what you learned in your dark place to bring others into the light. What God has spoken to us in challenging secret places is not meant just for us. Shout it from the rooftops!

#OutOfDarkness

Decree: I will listen in the dark! I will be bold in dark places! I hear God even when it's dark!

THE PUSH

Pray	Plan	Reflect

_____
_____
_____
_____
_____
_____
_____
_____
_____
_____
_____
_____
_____
_____
_____
_____
_____
_____
_____
_____
_____
_____
_____
_____
_____
_____
_____
_____
_____
_____

Day 105 The Cost
Luke 7:36-50

In the scripture above, Luke tells the story of the women with the alabaster box. Within the text it says that those who have been forgiven of much, love much. When you recognize the forgiving power of Christ it prevents you from judging others harshly. It causes you to love the Lord even more. People who perceive they are perfect cannot find a reason to kiss His feet, wash His feet with tears, or give up valuable oil. We should have no problem worshipping Jesus and make no apologies for our praise. Consider this all the huge mistakes we've made, the times we have doubted God, and the many experiences life brings (trials/tribulations), yet God still LOVES us. This woman was a sinner when she arrived. In fact, Jesus noted that her sins were many, yet she left forgiven. She had enough faith to pour out the oil from her alabaster box. She was called into question and others desired to prevent her quest, but through all that Jesus' choice was forgiveness. They didn't understand her actions because they did not have her testimony. God's choice for you today is the same; forgiveness. Pour out, worship Him, and give Him your best despite the accusations, religious walls, and cost. It is always worth it with God!

#TheCost

Decree: Nothing I have is greater than my worship! I will pursue God in the midst of those who don't understand. I will love and forgive with the same measure in which I have been forgiven and loved.

THE **PUSH**

Pray	Plan	Reflect

THE **PUSH**
Day 106 Overcoming Evil with Good
Romans 12:21

Romans 12:21," Be not overcome by evil, but overcome evil with good."

Evil is real and prevalent in the world. Revenge is often a flesh response when evil strikes, but it is not the way of God. The correct weapon to pull from our arsenal is not revenge, but good. Our response to evil should be to say something good, think good, and do good. We overcome evil with good, not more evil as the world often teaches.

We may view our life circumstances as evil. Life sometimes has a way of presenting challenges. When we experience any form of lack, attack, or evil in our lives, that is what should prompt us to sow into someone else's life. If you feel unloved, sow love. If you feel nobody cares, sow caring. Whatever you seek for yourself sow the same into someone else's life. When evil in your own life arises, use this as an opportunity to be a blessing and do good. We can overcome our own evils by doing something good for someone else. We can overcome the evil in the world by making goodness greater!

#GoodWins

Decree: I can overcome evil! The force of good is greater than any evil in my life! I will be good and do good!

THE PUSH

Pray	Plan	Reflect

_____
_____
_____
_____
_____
_____
_____
_____
_____
_____
_____
_____
_____
_____
_____
_____
_____
_____
_____
_____
_____
_____
_____
_____
_____
_____
_____
_____

Day 107 Not Window Shopping
Genesis 13:14-15

I have a confession to make. I do not enjoy window shopping. There are some people who can go to the mall or car dealership and walk around, just to see things with no intentions on buying anything. I have never enjoyed seeing things that I cannot have. There is good news! God does not give us window shopping, vision experiences. If He gives us the vision, He gives us the provision.

In Genesis 13:14-15 the Lord tells Abram to lift his eyes (your gaze should be directional and should not be down), look at the land (provision), because whatever you see (your vision), I am going to give you (determines what you will have). That is what God is telling you today. If you can look down at it, it is too small. You must look up and beyond your current circumstances and obstacles to the provision and vision God has given you. Before Abram could receive the land, he had to see it. Whatever Abram could see was pronounced by God. What do you see? Do you see yourself overcoming and acquiring? If not, you must take a different view. Look up! Everything God has shown you, you can have. See it!

Disclaimer: Notice that Abram is given land. The land itself does not grant wealth. God blesses Abram with provision, indicating that he has given him to get what he needs. It will still require work. Abram must work the land to make the vision worth having. Land without using the ground is meaningless. God has already given you the ability to access your prosperity through the provision.

#NotJustWindowShopping

Decree: Everything God showed me is mine! I can still see it! I am looking beyond my present circumstances.

THE PUSH

Pray	Plan	Reflect

Day 108 The Love Mandate
John 13:34

John 13:34 directs us to love one another the way Christ loves us. This may sound impossible to some. Love is especially difficult when we consider those who have hurt us. However, this scripture provides directions for getting on the path towards love. Here are some things to ponder: 1) consider how Christ loves you; 2) consider how unworthy you are of His love; 3) consider your sins; 4) consider the price He paid; and lastly, 5) consider where you would be without His love. Know that His grace and mercy are not just for you. FORGIVE and LOVE again. There is power in love! Many desire gifts and outwards signs of demonstrated power, but love is powerful for healing, deliverance, and your purpose. Love works, never fails, and is the greatest among the things we should desire (First Corinthians 13:13).

John 13:35 continues by telling us that everyone will know that we are a disciple of Christ by our love. Not by our gifts, talents, title, wise words, singing, preaching (you get it). We demonstrate that we are followers of Christ by our love. Often, we are looking for other manifestations and platforms to show we are mighty disciples. The world has tricked some to believe great discipleship is found in what we have, who we know, and the networks we travel. This scripture cautions us to not place any of these things before our actions of love. Our openness to share God's love towards us with others is the essential ingredient to showing the world that we follow Christ.

#Love

Decree: I understand the power of love. I will demonstrate God's love to others.

THE **PUSH**

Pray   **Plan**   **Reflect**

_____
_____
_____
_____
_____
_____
_____
_____
_____
_____
_____
_____
_____
_____
_____
_____
_____
_____
_____
_____
_____
_____
_____
_____
_____
_____
_____
_____

Day 109 Who Eats First?
Jeremiah 1:8-10 & Ezekiel 2:6-8

Jeremiah 1:8-10 and Ezekiel 2:6-8 combined tell us not to be afraid of men, their faces, their words, or their stares because God is with us. He tells the anointed and chosen to speak what he has given them without worrying about people. I believe this is because God knows that we are human and capable of placing too much emphasis on what people think of us, will say about us, and how they look at us. When God places a word in your mouth it is not subject to people's approval, only God's. I know all too well how easy it is to consider what people will think of us more than we consider what God will think. It is necessary to use wisdom and pray to God concerning the words we speak and the timing of our words. If the word is from God, it must be spoken even if it is uncomfortable.

God does not promise that people will not look at you crazy, will be receptive, and kind. He does not say that the weapons will not form, but He does say that they will not prosper (Isaiah 54:17). The text in Ezekiel indicates that there will be briers, thorns, and scorpions, yet God will be with us. Romans 8:31 tells us that if God be for us there is nothing worthy of even being mentioned as against us.

The word ministers even more, God tells Ezekiel to eat what I have given. These words are powerful because this means we must take in what God feeds us first, then give it to the people. Before we speak a word, we should chew on it, digest it, and apply it to our lives first. Then we will know it is palatable for the people.

#FirstPartakers

Decree: I will speak what God tells me to speak. I am not afraid of men and their faces. I will be the first partaker of the word.

THE **PUSH**

Pray	Plan	Reflect

_____

_____

_____

_____

_____

_____

_____

_____

_____

_____

_____

_____

_____

_____

_____

_____

_____

_____

_____

_____

_____

_____

_____

_____

_____

_____

_____

_____

Day 110 Closed Doors
John 20:19 & 26

In both John 20:19&26 the disciples of Jesus are gathered in fear. Jesus had been crucified and was no longer present with them. As they sat, Jesus entered the room through shut doors. We often pray for God to open doors. We know that He can open doors no man can shut (Revelation 3:8). However, closed doors can be a blessing. Do not let a closed door deter you from your destiny. Doors may look like obstacles to you, but we serve a God that can work through closed doors. Jesus declared greater works shall you do! The bible says in Mark 2:4 that when the four could not get the sick man to Jesus they took the roof off! Here is the revelation, you don't need an opened door. You need the faith to believe that even when obstacles are in your path they are not capable of destroying your God-given destiny. If you are meant to get in, God will create a window, build a door on your ceiling (your limitations). Take the roof off! The door is an excuse. A shut door just means there is more than one way to enter. The door is a physical limitation, but the spiritual realm is not limited by carnal obstacles. Transcend your limitation.

#Transcending

Decree: What God has assigned to me is mine! God will make a way for me. I am a creative thinker with limitless potential!

THE **PUSH**

Pray	Plan	Reflect

Day 111 Love & Friendship
First Corinthians 15:33, Proverbs 18:24 & 19:20

Why are you chasing what doesn't want to be caught?

I spent a large amount of my young adult years wanting everyone to like, approve, and be pleased with me. At times it took me out of my character, impacted my decision making, and led to compromises I have lived to regret. When people stopped calling, caring or supporting, I would go out of my way to find out what I did, try to fix it, seek reconnection and offer apologies…all just to find out later that the connections were never meant to be.

I have come to realize in the last decade (in my 30's-40's…a bit late) that we must seek God's approval and believe fully in His ability to connect us to the right people at the right time. While we should still desire love and peace with all, we no longer believe that means chasing a love that is fleeting. With a discerning eye, we must allow God to evaluate us and reflect on our actions. We must let go and let God so that we can walk in liberty. Maturity, discernment, and wisdom help guard us from games and manipulation. We must be delivered from guessing what we could have done to be thrown shade and spending too much time stuck in our imaginations. Real love does not leave you wondering. Real love affirms, corrects with compassion, and protects even when in pain. It is the way God love us. Simultaneously, we should remain teachable and ready to listen to any we have offended. That same heart allows us to sleep at night knowing that if we have an issue with someone we have addressed it and hope they would do the same.

You do not have to chase what wants you! The only people running from you are not for you! Chase God and you will meet some amazingly great people on the run!

THE **PUSH**

#RealFriends

Decree: I am surrounded by a powerful circle of Godly influence. I accept that some friendships are fleeting. I walk in love and peace with everyone, including myself.

Pray   **Plan**   **Reflect**

_____

_____

_____

_____

_____

_____

_____

_____

_____

_____

_____

_____

_____

_____

_____

_____

_____

_____

_____

_____

_____

_____

_____

_____

_____

_____

_____

_____

_____

_____

_____

Day 112 Lessons on Love & Time
First Peter 5:8

With all the talk of being a boss, hustling, and grinding, be sure to consider what all that means to those who love you! Early in ministry, I did a lot. I was busy all the time. After working 10-12 hours, showing up for everyone's events, living at the church because I was a part of all the organizations, I realized I left a door open in my home. Not a physical door. A spiritual door/void. It really does not matter what the opening was, it left a breach. When we ignore those, who love us we make room for the enemy. Your door may be the void your children feel, your spouse, family, or even yourself. Being busy does not equate to being productive. How much of you is left to give your spouse, friend, and family at the end of the day? Are you too tired from all the day's festivities to really enjoy your own company, your spouse, and children? Are you there, but thinking of your "to do list", on your cell phone, taking calls? What you love, you make time for, including yourself. When the rubber meets the road, those we take for granted most are usually the people who support us the most. When my family, friends, and husband speak the final words over me, I do not want it to be that I saved thousands while they died or starved for my attention. Not a single minute with those who love you and who you love is ever wasted. Let's put our time where our hearts are, reprioritize our lives, and commit to really making our families our first ministries. Tomorrow is not promised. If you love them, let them know today!

#FamilyFirst

Decree: I set aside time for my family, friends, and self. I am a good steward over my time. I am as successful privately as I am personally.

THE **PUSH**

Pray	Plan	Reflect

THE PUSH

Day 113 Can You Stand the Wind?
Ezekiel 17:8-10

Many people become upset at what the invisible force of wind does. Many blame the wind for the damage that we see. The wind is often accused of knocking down trees, power lines, signs, and roof singles. The wind is a power like no other because its force is often unseen, heard and witnessed by its effects. The wind is symbolic of the Holy Spirit. It moves, it's a force, in silence it demonstrates its power and strength. It builds, but also has the power to reveal weaknesses. The wind is often accused of knocking down things and destroying them, but things were weak before the wind showed up. We walked by them without knowing that their foundation was not stable, their roots were shallow, and their strength minimal. In those moments of ignorance, we were happy to oblige the weakness if it did not look the part. Then the wind comes and exposes the fantasy of stability. The storm pushes and beats on our wobbly support systems causing them to fall. We blame the wind, when we should be appreciative of its efforts to expose what we could not see without it. The storm, indeed, was not meant to break you, but to make you stronger. Once the weaknesses are exposed, we can fortify ourselves.

In the 1980's, an experiment was done to create an ecosystem in the desert housed under a dome. This ecosystem would include plants, a water system, and people. Scientists build it to simulate several different environments. They were able to successfully grow trees, however they noticed that the trees would only grow so high and then fall over. The trees were given all of the essential elements to survive; sun and water. Initially, the scientists were baffled and wondered what could cause this outcome. What they learned was the trees' roots were not deep and strong. Why? What prevented the trees from growing deep roots? The absence of wind! Wind causes the roots to be strengthen. The deeper the roots, the taller the tree can grow. We all want to show up tall, stable, and secure, but can you stand the wind? Let the winds of life fortify you.

238

THE **PUSH**

#LordSendTheWind

Decree: Lord, send the wind. God is revealing the things that are not secure in my life through my storms. I am fortified through life's trials. My roots are growing deeper. I am stronger after the wind.

THE **PUSH**

Pray	Plan	Reflect

THE **PUSH**

Day 114 Survival of the Fittest
Luke 17:11-19

Survival of the fittest is used to describe the adaptability of an organism to their environment. These organisms are considered the fittest because they continue to exist, while others become extinct due to changes in the environment. These organisms continue to thrive against all odds in changes to the climate and alterations in food supply. Why? Because they did not stick to what has always been, but instead adapted, changed, and created new ways to exist. They learned something new to survive.

To survive means to remain alive after a tragedy that killed others. It means you could have died in it, but you did not. It means you made it through when others died. If you are reading this page, I am sure you have survived. You have made it through pain, tears, darkness, loneliness, emptiness, and pain. You made it! But there is a difference among survivors.

There are two types of survivors. Those who made it because they were trained, qualified, and earned it. These survivors can tell you all about what THEY did to succeed. They can describe in detail the effort, hard work, and personal fortitude it required to survive. The other type of survivor cannot take credit for making it, arriving, or even being alive. This survival understands that they survived because they were rescued. Survivors that were rescued are grateful. They know how to send out an S.O.S, a sign of distress to God indicating they need help. Survivors that were rescued know how to get God's attention in worship, waving their hands, calling out to God with a loud voice, "I'm over here, I'm over here." They are not too proud to acknowledge that they cannot do it on their own. Another characteristic of a survivor who has been rescued is that they were helped. They were pulled out, carried, and bought to safety. They did not do it alone.

THE **PUSH**

The lepers in Luke 17 all survived. When they encountered Jesus, they were all healed and cleansed. They indeed survived being a leper, but only one understood he was rescued. Only one turned around and sent out an SOS of worship. He said, "Jesus, Master, have mercy on me." He turned back to say thank you, because he was unworthy. He understood he did not deserve to be cleansed and healed. He fell face down at Jesus' feet. Only one understood he was rescued. That also made him the fittest. He adapted to what just occurred in his life. He could no longer just follow the other nine lepers. He made a choice to adapt to what he experienced and adjusted his position to that of worship and thanksgiving. As a result, the leper was not just cleansed and healed, he was made whole. Only one was fit for the additional blessing.

If we want to be the fittest, we must acknowledge that we survived by the grace of God! We must go back and lay at His feet, thanking Him because we did not do it alone. Those who were rescued worshipped from a heart of gratitude that is unmatched by a mere survivor. Will you be the one who returns to worship?

#IWasRescued

Decree: I am grateful! I have made it, by the grace of God! I will honor God with my life. Jesus rescued me!

Pray　　　　　　　　　　**Plan**　　　　　　　　　　**Reflect**

Day 115: NO!
Matthew 5:37

When my children were younger, I had to say 'no' often. 'No' to candy before dinner. 'No' to walking away. 'No' to picking up things that had the potential to cause them harm. At times, my 'no's produced tears, attitudes, and disappointments, but I cared enough about my children to tell them 'no'. Not only are we wise enough to say no, but God as our Father knows when we need a 'no'. He closes doors. He says 'no' and sometimes "not right now" to protect us. When we can understand the need to say 'no' to our children and have experienced and understand a 'no' from God; why do we struggle to tell others 'no'?

Search your heart as it relates to being able to say 'no' to others. Having a sure 'no' is important. A sure 'no', prevents misunderstandings. It leaves no room for interpretation. A strong 'no' has finality to it. Why do we waiver?

Many of us are people pleasers. Like nurturers, caring, and helping, we sugar coat our conversations to keep from saying 'no'.,. If we give from a place of lack and starving ourselves of the fuel we need to help others, is that nurturing, caring, and/or helping? If we end up down because we cannot say 'no', we cause a cycle of need to occur. In no way should we be selfish individuals who never care or express concern for others. We should not negate self-care to gain friendships, loyalty, or approval from others. What motivates us to do well or good for others is just as important as the act itself. Saying 'no' to other things, is sometimes saying yes to ourselves. Consider your schedule, what obstacles get in the way of you accomplishing your personal goals or being in great physical, emotional, and mental health. What can you do to alleviate the pressure to say 'yes', when you should say NO? Where does that need to say yes originate?

THE **PUSH**

Mothers and fathers with all the love and care they have for their children, still say 'no'. Our Heavenly Father, who is love and who has a plan to prosper us, still says 'no'. Who are we not to say 'no'? Practice saying NO today!

#ASureStrongNO!

Decree: I love me enough to say 'no' to things that deplete me. My love is not just demonstrated in my yes. My NO is sure. Today, I say YES to me and 'no' to people pleasing.

THE **PUSH**

Pray   **Plan**   **Reflect**

Day 116: The Come Back - Victorious
Judges 16

Samson was a strong man. He was known for his capacity to gain victory by using physical strength. Samson was also born with a frailty. His strength was hair dependent. Do not get too caught up in the fact that Samson's strength was in his hair. We all have what some will consider natural strengths, things we were born with or seem to have had all our lives. We may instinctively depend on that strength to help us out in difficulties. This can also lead us to have a false sense of our strength. Much like Samson who was strong physically, but spiritually weak. When Delilah was sent by his enemies to discover Samson's weakness, he took great pleasure in demonstrating his physical strength. She was plotting to discover his true weakness and relentlessly pursued it until it was revealed. Learning that his strength was in his hair, she informed the Philistines and they shaved his head and took his eyes. However, she missed one critical detail. Hair grows back! Samson regained his strength and avenged what was done to him. God will restore you! Whatever you lose, through Christ, you can grow it back! I see the beginning of a comeback.

#MakingAComeBack

Decree: I see new growth in my life. I believe God can replace whatever I have lost. I expect to come back from this!

THE **PUSH**

Pray	Plan	Reflect

_____

_____

_____

_____

_____

_____

_____

_____

_____

_____

_____

_____

_____

_____

_____

_____

_____

_____

_____

_____

_____

_____

_____

_____

_____

_____

_____

THE **PUSH**

Day 117: Give Me My Goliath
First Samuel 17:19-26

First Samuel tells the story of a giant Philistine that taunts the people of Israel. David becomes the hero of the text and takes down Goliath. Here is a reminder of David's background. At this time, Saul was the current king, however God sent Samuel to anoint a new king. Samuel visits the house of Jesse (David's father) in pursuit of the next king. Jesse brings out all his sons as possibilities but does not bring out David. The prophet Samuel determines that none of the sons that Jesse brought out was the chosen one. Finally, David is found shepherding the sheep and is confirmed to be the one Samuel was seeking. Samuel anoints David. Now David is anointed for a calling that is already occupied, but God was no longer with Saul. David comes to the stand-off between the Philistines and Israel to find Goliath defying the army of God (Israel). David becomes curious about Goliath and interested in why no one has attempted to kill him.

In the text, Goliath represents a giant obstacle, an opportunity to show and prove, and a call to action. Every good leader has a Goliath experience. When Goliath is handled correctly it brings private success to the public eye, exposes a King/Queen, and restores honor to God.

David was an anointed unknown. He had been called by God, but nobody knew who he was, until Goliath. When Goliath came into David's life it was an opportunity for David to make what he had accomplished in private, public. The bible tells us in verse 50 that David privately killed a bear and a lion to protect the lamb. They did not know David's resume, but he was aware of his capabilities. We must reflect on what we have accomplished in private. God will require us to do His will in private, before ever making it public. Without Goliath, we would not know David's ability to fight and rescue. It would have remained his secret. If you are reading this, it is likely that God can shift you from private success to public success.

Through David's experience with Goliath, we find out he already has leadership abilities. David reveals king-like characteristics. First, he was willing to risk his life for a sheep, for those he led. Second, he seeks to kill Goliath not because he wants to demonstrate his power, but because Goliath defied the army of the living God. David's stance was for God. David won a victory not just for him, but for a nation. Goliath was David's opportunity to show who he was and his preparation to be king. Goliath was not a problem; he was a promotion.

How will you view your obstacle?

#GiveMeMyGoliath

Decree: Give me my Goliath! This obstacle is a promotion. After this, there is victory.

THE **PUSH**

Pray	Plan	Reflect

THE **PUSH**

Day 118: He Covers Me
Psalms 27:5 & Psalms 91

The story of Adam and Eve reveals a truth of our sinful nature. We will attempt to cover ourselves when we have fallen. However, God heals what He covers, not what we hide. God covers us in many ways. Let's address four ways. 1) God paid the price for our sins. He covered the cost we should have paid. 2) He protects us from visible and invisible dangers. He keeps us from the snares of the enemy. 3) He hides us. God is a secret place that the enemy cannot infiltrate. When we are in His presence and under His authority the enemy is unable to find us. 4) He sees us. Like a watchman or a "look-out", God is observing our movement and all things concerning us. He is aware. He sees us.

Be glad you serve a God who paid the price, protects, hides, and looks out for us. Stay covered! How do you stay hidden and covered? You must believe in God's power to save and cover you even at your weakest moments. God does not use our vulnerability to expose us, but to cover us. In your moments of weakness do not run from His grace, mercy, and forgiveness, let it cover you. Let God's love overcome you. Let His blood wash you. He's got you covered.

#CoverMe

Decree: Lord, cover me! Lord thank you for paying what I owed. Lord protect me. Lord hide me. Jesus look out for me.

THE **PUSH**

Pray	Plan	Reflect

THE **PUSH**

Day 119: Tools You Can Use
John 19:17 & Matthew 16:24

Tools are used to solve problems, fix, or build things. The right tool helps us do things easier, prevents further damage, and often saves time, energy, and effort. Given a list of tools, we would likely be able to name the occupation. The same should be true for us as Christians. As Christians some of our basic tools are prayer, fasting, and studying the word. The enemy would love for us to never use our tools. He attempts to convince you that they don't really work. The enemy further tries to convince YOU that you don't know how to use the tools and the tools are not as big as or is not a match for your problem. He understands that if we ascribe to this way of thinking; don't pray, study, or fast; his victory is inevitable. We must use the tools we were given. They make life easier, save us time and energy, and prevent further damage because they are the right tools for the assignment/job we are facing. Our job is not just to defeat the enemy but build the kingdom of God and live life in abundance.

Jesus was a carpenter. This means His early work was performed by cutting, shaping, and installing building materials during construction. Jesus uses the same tools to cut/prune, shape/mold, and build us up that He used and specialized on Calvary. Carpenters are skilled in working with nails and wood. Jesus did His best work on Calvary and used the tools of a carpenter to do it. What tools do you already have? Consider David. He could not use Saul's armor, he used what he already knew and was proven, 5 smooth stones and a sling shot. Jesus used what He knew would get the job done. Both were led to victory because they used the right tools. Use your tools! Do not sit there with your tool box complaining that nothing is being built. Use every tool God has given you from experiences, through prayer, fasting, and decreeing God's word over your life. He gave you the tools, build with them!

#UseYourTools

THE **PUSH**

Decree: I will dust off my tools. The enemy cannot and shall not win. My tools work. I am capable of effectively using the things God has given me.

THE **PUSH**

Pray	Plan	Reflect

Day 120: Don't Forget About Me
Genesis 8:1, Genesis 19:29, Genesis 30:22, First Samuel 1:19, Jeremiah 31:20 & Psalms 105:42

In our fast-paced world of hustle and bustle everyone is so busy. It's a struggle to make time for friends and family. This type of busyness often causes us to forget those we care about. We may forget birthdays, anniversaries, or even miss making calls to our loved ones.

The above text emphasized God's amazing ability to remember us. He remembers Noah, Abraham, Hannah, Ephraim, and Rachel. Each text reads and the Lord/God remembered (insert name). And He remembers you too.

Every time you have prayed, sacrificed, and obeyed--God remembers. Even in the face of adversity as in the case of Hannah and Rachel, He remembers. He remembered the faith of Noah, the obedience of Abraham, and the repentance of Ephraim! He remembers your prayers, tears, and all you have endured for the cross. He has not forgotten you. He is the great El Roi, the God who sees. He is also omniscient, He knows everything. He's got you! He has not forgotten His promise to you. He remembers!

#GodRemembersMe

Decree: Thank you for being omniscient and concerned about me Lord. You are a God who does not forget. You have not forgotten about me. You will fulfill every promise concerning me. You see me and remember me.

THE **PUSH**

Pray	Plan	Reflect

THE **PUSH**
BONUS

Day 121: Push
John 16:21

Pregnancy in the natural shares similarities with being spiritually pregnant. When someone is spiritually pregnant they will not give birth to a baby, but rather a vision, promise, or revelation. With both pregnancies when it gets close to the due date/due season the pressure increases. As we count down the hours and minutes the pressure intensifies and becomes painful. The pain and pressure have a purpose. They both get so unbearable, you are forced to push. Pushing relieves the pressure, but not the pain. At some point you make up your mind that you want the pain to end and the only way to get there is to push. It will demand focus, effort, stamina, and perseverance. It will not ask for them, it will demand them. You will be given no choice, but to push. This is not the time to change your mind, even if you wanted to your body/spirit will not let you. At this point, all other options are null and void. It is your time, your moment to push. It won't be easy, but it will be worth it. John 16:21 points out a truth as it relates to giving birth. Once the process is complete, we are so engrossed with the beauty of the result, the once unbearable pain is not even a thought. It's your time and season to birth what God has given you. Push!

#PUSH

Decree: I am pushing and pressing towards my mark. I am pushing through. My pain and the pressure have a beautiful purpose. The blessing will far outweigh the pain.

THE PUSH

Pray   Plan   Reflect

_____

_____

_____

_____

_____

_____

_____

_____

_____

_____

_____

_____

_____

_____

_____

_____

_____

_____

_____

_____

_____

_____

_____

_____

_____

_____

_____

THE **PUSH**
Pastor Margo M. Gross

Pastor Margo M. Gross was born in Washington, DC and now resides in southern Maryland with her husband and two daughters. Margo is a product of both the District of Columbia and the Calvert County Public School systems. After graduating, she earned a Bachelor of Science Degree from the University of Maryland Eastern Shore and a Master of Arts in Teaching from Trinity Washington University. She is a member of Alpha Kappa Alpha Sorority Incorporated and Fierce Ladies Achieving Ministry and Entrepreneurial Success (FLAMES).

Margo has been an educator in the public-school system in the Washington Metropolitan areas and suburbs for almost 20 years. She has won numerous awards in the educational arena including Calvert County Teacher of the Year and Outstanding Educator from the Concerned Black Women of Calvert County. Mrs. Gross is currently a school administrator and is pursuing her PhD in Educational Leadership.

Margo's passion for education is only exceeded by her love for ministry. Pastor Gross has been a minister of the gospel for 20 years. As the Senior Pastor of The Remnant of Hope International Church in Maryland, Pastor Gross seeks to challenge people to live better, equip them to disciple, and make a positive impact in the community they serve. Her ministry gift has taken her around the country as well as Trinidad in both educational and ministerial arenas. Margo Gross is the founder of Margo Medina Ministries which provides mentorship and motivation through her life changing PUSH series and gives back to the Community through the Random Occasions of Care and Kindness (ROCK) Outreach.

Pastor Gross is known for her hands-on approach to leadership development, her transparent delivery of God's word, and her anointing to impart revelation to those who struggle to understand God's word. Pastor Gross is committed to fulfilling God's purpose in her life by empowering

THE **PUSH**

and inspiring others to desire a personal relationship with Jesus. It is Pastor Gross's desire to change lives through the word of God and she does so with humility, compassion, and integrity.

For bookings please email margomedina@verizon.net
Follow Pastor Gross on Facebook @Margo Medina Ministries
Instagram @Margo_Medina

262

THE **PUSH**

Made in the USA
Columbia, SC
26 May 2019